SHINE THROUGH YOUR STORY

REKINDLE Your Purpose, IGNITE Your Light & ILLUMINATE the World by SHARING YOUR STORY

MICHELLE PRINCE

ISBN:
Softcover: 978-1-956914-81-8
Hardcover: 978-1-956914-17-7
eBook: 978-1-956914-80-1
Library of Congress Control Number: 2023904939

CONTENTS

PRAISE FOR SHINE THROUGH YOUR STORY

"Have you ever felt like your story isn't worth sharing or that you aren't able to tell it in a compelling way? SHINE Through Your Story *will convince you otherwise. God has created each one of us in His image, and since He is the ultimate Creator, He has shared that creativity with all of us. Michelle will show you how to make sure your light is shining bright!"*

Jordan Raynor
Bestselling Author of *The Creator in You*
and *Called to Create*

One of the major themes of my books is that your stories matter! In SHINE Through Your Story, *Michelle Prince shares a formula to help identify your purpose, ignite your light and shine through your story for God's glory.*

Bob Beaudine
National Bestselling Author of *The Power of WHO*
and *2 Chairs*

"The most powerful story in the world is the story you tell yourself. Why? Because the story you tell yourself either limits or unleashes your ability to SHINE and impact others for good. Read SHINE Through Your Story *today—someone is desperately waiting to hear your story, and Michelle Prince shows you WHY your story is so important and HOW to share it!"*

Tom Ziglar
CEO, Ziglar Inc.
Proud Son of Zig Ziglar

"Even though I have known Michelle for many years, as I read this book, I found myself truly inspired. I laughed. I cried. And I cheered as Michelle shares with others how to SHINE! I can't wait to get my signed copy!"

Howard Partridge
President, Phenomenal Products, Inc.

In SHINE Through Your Story, *Michelle makes a compelling case for the power of our stories to transform lives. I love how she equips you with the foundational tools to help you discover and share your own story while simultaneously modeling it by sharing hers. Don't casually read this book. Let it ignite you as you encounter God's goodness on the pages within it.*

Shae Bynes
Co-Founder of Kingdom Driven Entrepreneur
and Author of *Grace Over Grind*

"When Michelle Prince walks into a room, the atmosphere changes. She is not only beautiful, but warm, gracious, kind, and very intelligent. I am so excited about her new book SHINE Through Your Story. She has a way to encourage and inspire you. So many people give up on their dreams and begin to doubt their calling and purpose. Michelle shares how we all are important and challenges us to tell our story. Your story matters, and someone needs to hear it. God has given you a platform and an influence that are unique to you. This book is going to be a bestseller, and you will be transformed by reading it. I am honored to call Michelle Prince my friend."

Judy Pogue
Co-founder, Pouge Constructions
and Pogue Missions

"I've read no more convincing persuasion as it relates to writing and publishing your story for the good of others than SHINE Through Your Story. Michelle Prince's book is written as she speaks: in a conversational and honestly transparent style. Whether you've ever even considered writing your story—or if you simply need a gentle nudge to do so—this book will be your deciding factor. Enjoy the write!!!"

Laurie Magers
Executive Assistant to Zig and Tom Ziglar

"Michelle's passion and purpose SHINE through in this amazing book. With step-by-step guiding points to help you find your passion and ample encouragement to help you share those gifts through your story, this book is an exceptional tool to use and give to those you care for. I'm so excited to see how many lives are positively impacted by this heartfelt and power-packed book. Thank you, Michelle!"

Cheri Perry
MVP Director, TMC

"It can be difficult to believe your story matters when your experiences are filled with shame. However, the reality is your darkest moments can be the light of hope for others to realize their stories matter too. SHINE Through Your Story equips you to turn your most difficult life experiences into your greatest life purpose."

LeTesha Wheeler
Author, *Half Breed – Finding Unity in a Divided World*

I've known Michelle Prince for over 20 years, and in every book, interaction, and engagement, she gives her heart and her all to help others realize their goals. SHINE Through Your Story *is a blueprint to help move you from fear to purpose as you share your story to bring God glory! I believe this is Michelle's most transparent and poignant work to date. I hope every believer will get their hands on this book to help us spread the good news around the world!*

Jill Hellwig
Founder/CEO Brand New U Coaching, Ziglar Legacy Certified Trainer & Coach, Author of *Grow with Goals* and Co-Author of *When Women Reign*

The world is full of darkness and desperately needs people born of the Light to shine theirs for others, but too many have become comfortable sitting on their couches, binging Netflix. Michelle's timely words will awaken sleeping giants to recognize the seeds of greatness planted in them. Reading her book makes you want to get up and take action with a renewed sense of purpose. Her practical formula and personal stories provide the road map to greatness. Let Revival begin within the hearts of each person who reads this book.

Kim Gilson
Writer, Teacher, Speaker
Excellivate, "Activating the Excellence in You"
www.excellivate.com

Michelle's vulnerable and heartfelt message of helping others shine through telling their stories "shines" through this book, SHINE Through Your Story. *Using her own story of insecurity and questioning what she has to offer, which many women struggle with, she provided the backdrop of how God used her and her story to help thousands of others tell theirs. This book will help you decide to tell your story and let God shine through you.*

Tanya Hendrix
Lawyer and Author of *Equal Protection Under God* and *Seen*

SHINE Through Your Story *can open the door of your faith, reignite it and possibly open the door to a new career path. My precious dad sadly passed away before the book was launched. Learning through Michelle's book and Zig Ziglar's teachings has helped me a lot. Let us all show love while we can.*

C. Rampellini & Family

This book is changing my life and perspective! The refreshing sense of hope and purpose you create in the book is helping to reignite my passion for sharing my story and is shifting my thinking exponentially. Thank you!

Gary Wilkin
Founder of My Retirement Mission

I needed to read this book for so many reasons. It touched my soul and I am so grateful and honored to know you, Michelle. This book is a gift and so are you! Thank you for sharing your story and for motivating, inspiring, and encouraging me and so many others.

Joanie Bily
Chief Workforce Analyst, Employbridge and Author of *Dive In D.E.E.P.*

If you have ever wanted to write a book, you must start by reading this book! Michelle has shared her life story and given us precise details on how to begin writing your story. I have followed Michelle for 8 years and have been to several of her Book Bound conferences. She is genuinely passionate in her approach, motivation, and love of helping others! SHINE Through Your Story *will be a bestseller!*

Kathryn M Pistoresi
Founder/CEO of Physique Fitness Therapy
Author of *20 Minutes to Live*

The timing of the release of Michelle Prince's highly anticipated next book, SHINE Through Your Story, *could not be better. Currently, there are many challenging issues in our world. Michelle's well-thought-out book is absolutely refreshing and inspiring. Her message and methods for finding one's own story are clearly communicated with exercises to guide the reader. I have known Michelle as a motivational speaker, writer, and publisher with a sincere and knowledgeable approach. Michelle has carved out a unique niche for herself. Although she has worked with some of the best in the business, she is a motivator for a new day, relying on the BEST expert of all, God Almighty, for her direction and guidance. I am honored to have received an advanced copy to read and to have as a resource in my own personal library.*

Mary Yana Burau
CEO of ItsAGreatDayTo.com and
Author of *It's a Great Day To...Gather Around a Table*

Chapter One

This Little Light of Mine

"Live as children of light..."
(Ephesians 5:8)

I am not sure how old I was when I first heard this song, but I remember it always making me smile. It was so easy to sing, and it went something like this, *"This little light of mine, I'm gonna let it shine. This little light of mine, I'm gonna let it shine. This little light of mine, I'm gonna let it shine. Let it shine, let it shine, let it shine!"*

It still makes me smile, even singing it now. And how easy is it for all of us to understand what it's about? We're supposed to shine our light ... be the light for others. We're supposed to illuminate the light that's been given to us by God.

Yet it never really occurred to me, until just now, that part of this song is missing. You see, it says, *"This little light of mine, I'm gonna let it shine."* But what if you don't know what your light is? What if you don't think you even have a light to shine? What if that light has been extinguished by hard times, difficulties, and tragedy? And what if the thought of that light ever burning bright again seems so, so far away?

I'm here to tell you that you do have a light. Your light is your story. Your light is what God has created in you. It is your purpose. It is why you are here. And the reason we have a light—the reason we have a story to share—is because God wants us to shine through it. He doesn't want us to extinguish it, to be afraid to light it up again. He wants us to figure out what that light is and let it shine.

> **Your light is your story. Your light is what God has created in you.**

WHAT'S YOUR LIGHT?

Before we can shine outward though, we must look inward. How can we shine a light that we don't even know exists? How can we make a difference in the world when we're still unsure about ourselves? I know this feeling all too well. You'll hear more about my story later in the book, but if you're anything like me, you don't want to be burned out. You don't want to flicker and fade. You want to shine brightly. You want to be the reason somebody smiles. You want to be the reason somebody's life is better. You want to be the reason people are drawn to your light, which is the light of Christ.

But how can we make a difference for God if we're too afraid to light the very light He gave us?

You see, our light is our life, and our life is the story that we've been given. No matter what's happened to you, you can still choose to shine. You can choose to shine through the pain, the tears, the fear, the uncertainty. You can realize that your story (your light) is how we bring glory to God. And the only way others will be attracted to our light is when we shine.

I love the analogy of a flashlight in a dark room. Have you ever been in a situation when the power went out and you find yourself in a pitch-black room? It's so dark that you literally can't even see the hand in front of you. But when you turn on your flashlight or light a match, the world around you instantly becomes illuminated. Suddenly, you can find your way. The darkness is gone.

How is that possible? Here's what I know to be true: light will always defeat darkness. Always! No matter how much darkness surrounds you or how many things have happened to you, all it takes is a one flicker of light to illuminate your path. One ounce of light penetrates the darkness every single time.

If you're reading this book, then you're probably like me—you strive to live purposely. You want to know what that God-given purpose is and how to live it out fully. You want to know that your purpose matters... that *you* matter. You want to create real impact that lives on.

Friend, I'm here to tell you that you and your purpose do matter. You are here on this earth for a reason. You were designed to shine. And when you do, you will glorify God with your light.

REIGNITE YOUR LIGHT

There was a time in my life when I felt so burned out. I felt like I had literally nothing left to give to any of the people in my life.

But deep down, I knew what I had to do. I mean, I'd heard the announcement a thousand times on airplanes, so how could I not know? You know the one where they tell you, "In case of emergency, put your oxygen mask on first so that you can assist a child or someone else in need." I knew I had to take care of myself first, but I spent many years doing exactly the opposite.

I'm a mom, wife, friend, daughter, and more. So naturally, I wanted to excel in all those roles. I gave and gave and gave, but sometimes to the detriment of myself. Yes, the sacrifices I made were great—I'm not suggesting that giving to others is a bad thing. We're all called to serve. But when you give so much and don't put anything back for yourself, if you don't fill your own cup up, how can you pour it out for anyone else?

> When you truly understand who you are, your purpose, where that light comes from, and the purpose behind shining it, it can never be extinguished.

When you truly understand who you are, your purpose, where that light comes from, and the purpose behind shining it, it can never be extinguished.

Let me show you what I mean. Imagine you're holding a candle with the flame burning bright. Meanwhile, you have a second unlit candle on the table in front of you. If you were to take the lit candle and light the wick of the second candle, does the fire from the first candle burn out? No. The flame stays just as bright.

Now imagine you take that same first candle and light a third, fourth, and even a fifth candle. Would the lighting of multiple candles extinguish the original flame? Of course not! Why? Because the light from the first candle, the original source of the light, can never run out. The light only creates more light out in the world.

I explained this analogy to my oldest son, Austin, when he was three years old. At the time I was pregnant with our second child, Tyler, and Austin wasn't too excited about having to share my attention with anyone else. He really loved being an only child, and he was worried that having another child in the house would take away some of the love I had for him. Or if I'm totally honest, maybe I was the one who was worried about that. I mean, how could I possibly have enough love in my heart for two kids when I loved my one so much? Thankfully, having Tyler filled my love tank more than I could have ever imagined. The candlelight analogy helped Austin to understand that another child doesn't take away any love from him, it just creates more love.

You are light. I am light. And when we share that light, we brighten and illuminate the world for others. It doesn't take away anything from us. In fact, I know that when I give out my light, when I shine the brightest, I feel the happiest. So, in sharing our light, in sharing our story, it's not about us … it's about others. Once you know what your light is, and once you know your purpose, and once you know the gifts that God has given you, then it's not scary to shine.

> **But when you do find your purpose in life, it doesn't matter *when* you get clarity. It only matters that you do.**

But how do you first light your own candle? How does that fire ignite?

I believe it comes by first figuring out who you are, what you want, and why God made you. Later in the book, I'll walk you through more of my journey, but just know I didn't wake up one day knowing my purpose. In fact, I struggled most of my life. I'm not going to say I am even fully aware of what my biggest purpose is yet. I'm still trying to figure out what my light is for, and how I'm supposed to ignite it in greater ways. But when you *do* find your purpose in life, it doesn't matter when you get clarity. It only matters that you do.

THE POWER OF YOUR STORY

Can you think of a story you've read or heard that struck you all the way down to your core and changed your entire perspective on life? Think about what that one story meant to you. It may have been a story about someone who reached a goal by overcoming their fear. Maybe it was a story about someone overcoming cancer—giving you hope that it could be your story as you or a loved one are sitting in a chair waiting to get chemo for the first time. It may be a story of a business owner who lost everything after the recession but was able to build another business twice as profitable as the one they lost.

What was that one story for you, and why did it have such a profound impact on your life?

Maybe, just maybe, for another person, that one story is *your* story. Maybe your life experiences, the moments that make up the story of your life, can create the most profound impact on another—maybe a beloved family member or someone you've never even met. Stories matter! Stories save! Stories can bring new life into this crazy, unsettling world!

Marketing companies capture your attention daily through their stories of others persevering, giving you hope that you can too—well, if you would just buy the product they are selling! They understand the power of a good story. Do you? Do you understand the power you have within you at this very moment? Do you understand the power of *your* story?

What is the one thing … the one lesson … the one gem that you wish you could share with the world to make it a better place? What nugget of wisdom do you have that can save others from making a huge mistake, or ease someone's pain in their journey of life? Your life's journey, your story, can create real impact in the life of future generations for many years to come. How cool does that sound? Yet, the impact won't be felt unless it is heard or otherwise shared.

Only you can bring more into the lives of others by revealing how you got to where you are in life, how you persevered, how you won in life, or how you are winning now! This book will give you the key steps on how to create more hope, love, healing, and positivity in this world … through your story, starting today!

A lot of people are going through life searching for hope, understanding, and more meaning. They are looking for answers! Maybe those answers can be found through *your* words, providing reassurance that they are not alone. There is someone else out there just like them—someone in pain or feeling lost.

I chose to share my story through writing and speaking—as I was called to do. If my path is not your path, don't let that deter you from reading on. I think you will find we each have our own path, and by reading my story, which God put directly in your path at this exact moment in time, your own calling can and will be further illuminated.

YOUR STORY IS A GIFT

You have a story, and your story matters. Your story is part of your purpose, and God gave it to you for a reason. He gave you your story to serve His purpose, to glorify Him, and to use it to serve others. Your story is a gift, and gifts are always meant to be shared.

There are many ways to tell your story. You could write it, speak it, share it on a video or podcast, or communicate it through one-on-one coaching, in a Bible study, or just over coffee. How you share your story isn't as important as knowing that you have a story to tell and that you are called to give the gift of your story to someone who needs it.

> You cannot change the history of your story – those things that are in the past. But what if your story influenced someone else's future? What if your story played a bigger part in His story?

Some parts of your story may be positive and uplifting, while other parts may have been difficult or traumatic. You may not have asked for it, but nonetheless, it's *your* story.

You cannot change the *history* of your story—those things that are in the past. But *what if* your story influenced someone else's *future*? *What if* your story played a bigger part in *His* story? *What if* putting your pen to paper played a big part in your own future? Okay, no more "what ifs" for your life ... let's change the terminology to *when* you share your story. *When* you change your life and that of another! It is all about WHEN now!

If parts of your story are messy, that's OK! Because in your mess is your message, and in your test is your testimony. You can share your story and turn your setback into a setup for someone else! So, if you want to serve others ... if you want to make a difference in this world, then you simply must tell your story.

How do I know? My entire life changed after following the nudge to tell my story and write my first book, **Winning In Life Now**. It's one of the reasons why I'm so passionate about helping others to tell their stories now—because I've seen firsthand what can happen when you do.

To share your story, you first must believe that your story matters. Do you *really* believe that your story matters? I hope so, because people will believe in you to the exact degree that you believe in yourself. So, if you believe that you have something valuable to share—that your story can help someone else—then they will believe in you too.

> **People will believe in you to the exact degree that you believe in yourself.**

Of course, the opposite is also true. If you believe your story and your light are *not* worthy of sharing, then, unfortunately, others will believe that too. Either way, it all starts with you! Don't let this discourage you or get you down. Even if you are not feeling worthy yet, you will hear stories and anecdotes all throughout this book to help you see the beauty already within you.

What's important is that we find a way to believe in ourselves, instead of surrendering ourselves to fears that stop us from seeing the greatness God put within each and every one of our souls. God placed *seeds of greatness* within us before we even took our first breath.

I fully believe that we have the power to impact people's lives through our stories—the power to inspire, encourage, and equip others to be all they were created to be. But, like Uncle Ben said to Peter Parker in the movie Spider-Man, "With great power comes great responsibility."

THE SIN OF THE DESERT

My friend Tom Ziglar shared an impactful story with me that really brings home this point. We're not sure who originally wrote it, but it's called "The Sin of the Desert."

Imagine that you're in the desert, and it's *hot*! People around you are literally dying of thirst. It's a horrible situation.

But the good news is you found water! You know how to quench the thirst for yourself and literally save the lives of all the people around you.

But what if you chose not to tell them? What if you kept that critical information just for yourself? What if you let them die when you knew what they needed to live? That would be a sin. So, the "sin of the desert" is when you know where the water is, but you refuse to tell others.

You're probably thinking, *I'd never do that!* I thought that too, but the reality is we do this every day. We do this when we keep our stories to ourselves—the same stories that could inspire or give hope and encouragement to a thirsty soul.

My goal with this book is to help you find the confidence in yourself, in your story, and in your ability to share it with others. Even if it's just for one other person, your story can mean the world to them. That one person could be YOU!

There are people in this world who are desperate to hear what you have to say. I pray that you boldly step out in faith, tell your story, and have the courage to shine your light. You can make a difference and inspire others to do the same.

You may be thinking—why me? I am not special. I'll counter with this: Why *not* you? I am here to tell you that, as God's uniquely and perfectly designed children, we are *all* special! We are all His masterpiece. He put us here in exactly this time and place in the universe. We are here to have impact … to take action … and most importantly, to shine! And God equips those He calls so we can accomplish the work He's called us to do.

As you consider what story you will share, envision the joy you will feel when you change just one heart to see a brighter pathway toward God. I can tell you from experience that nothing feels better than knowing you helped one person gain clarity into how they can impact the world by illuminating their light. You see, God is the original source of all creativity, so your work will compound all that He has given to this world. Just you. Just your story. Just your words—from His words to you!

> **We are here to have impact... to take action... and most importantly, to shine!**

My hope for you is that your inner spark gets re-ignited, and you become all that you were created to be. Because when that little light of yours lights the world for someone else, oh, the joy that comes with that! And that joy comes not just from singing the song … it comes by living the song. *"This little light of mine, I'm gonna let it shine … Let it shine, let it shine, let it shine!"*

CHAPTER TWO

YOUR STORY MATTERS

"You are the light of the world. A town built on a hill cannot be hidden. Neither do people light a lamp and put it under a bowl. Instead they put it on its stand, and it gives light to everyone in the house. In the same way, let your light shine before others, that they may see your good deeds and glorify your Father in heaven."
(Matthew 5:14-16)

According to the most recent United Nations estimates, there are over 8 billion people in this world. Yet each one of us has our own beliefs, knowledge, experiences, challenges, passions, values, thoughts, and ideas that can inspire, give hope, and teach others. We are all unique ... right down to our very own original fingerprint and DNA!

> **We have been Divinely created for greatness. Our path has been laid out perfectly according to His purpose for us.**

We have been Divinely created for greatness. Our path has been laid out perfectly according to His purpose for us. With the gifts we have been given comes a responsibility to share our greatness with the world for His benefit. We all hear the dire stories all over social media, in the movies, and on the news. God has created a way for us to fight evil with good ... to fight the negative messages of the day with messages of perseverance, hope, and love. Our goodness can prevail through spreading our messages far and wide. We must remember why we have our gifts… to help others.

"Now to each one the manifestation of the Spirit
is given for the common good."
(1 Corinthians 12:7)

When you think about it from that perspective, there can be literally hundreds, thousands, or even millions of other people in this world who want to know what you know or how to do something that you already know how to do. Even sharing a different perspective can change the life of another or create a sense of hope where there wasn't any.

… Maybe they want information on a subject that you have a deep knowledge and burning passion about.

… Or maybe they are going through a hardship right now, one that perhaps you have also dealt with. Maybe they are looking for resources and relationships to help them know that they are not alone. Your story can comfort them with the knowledge that they are not the first person to experience such loss, trials, or difficulties. You can show them that prevailing is an option.

… Maybe you have a special talent that has taken you years to master. If so, I bet you there's someone out there that would benefit from hearing about your experiences and lessons learned … if only it was available.

… You might be a business owner or service professional who has experienced tremendous success or has an exceptional background. If that's the case, I bet you there are other professionals out there who would like to learn from you so they can be successful too.

But aside from just teaching someone what you know, imagine:

- *What if your story was the turning point for someone else to make a positive change in their life?*

- *What if your story helped someone to finally overcome an addiction, heal a broken relationship, or achieve a lifelong goal?*

- *What if your story was the one thing that gave someone hope when they were feeling down or discouraged and needed it most?*

- *What if your story kept someone from committing self-harm or hurting others?*

- *What if your story inspired someone to take action because they thought, "If she can do it, I can do it!"*

- *What if just one person read your story and it made a total difference in their life?*

What if that one person was you? Would you write it? I believe we would all want to share our stories if we knew it would help someone else. Even better, what if it helped you clear out the clutter in your own brain by writing it out?

> **Deep down, don't we all want to make a difference, feel significant, and know that we matter—that our stories matter?**

Deep down, don't we all want to make a difference, feel significant, and know that we matter—that our stories matter? I know I do, and I think you do too, or you wouldn't be reading this book.

But sometimes sharing our stories can seem intimidating, or even pointless. After all, who really cares, right? At least that is how I felt. But when you see it from the perspective of giving hope to someone who may need encouragement to keep pushing forward, then it makes it all the more worthwhile ... and necessary.

The History of Stories

Jesus told stories. The apostles told stories. It's because those stories were written down in what we now have as the Bible that we even know about them today. The Holy Spirit's work through the church, as documented in the Bible, is what is responsible for making believers today.

If the disciples had walked with Jesus but kept those stories to themselves, we wouldn't be living today with the hope that we have in the Truth. We would not have so many of the answers that we seek.

> **It's about sharing your story and shining His light through your story for others to see.**

You see, it's not just about your story. It's about *sharing* your story and shining His light *through* your story for others to see. He has called you for this day and time. As we know, God is with us every step of the way. He always shows up in His perfect way and just on time! He created you to live prosperously with joy in your heart.

You Were Created to SHINE

You are loved, favored, and chosen to serve a higher purpose and to glorify God in the process. You are His masterpiece, created in His image to shine His light through you. There is power in you being you, the real you. If you don't believe me, believe His words, as shared in Ephesians 2:10 (NLT):

> *"For we are God's masterpiece. He has created us anew in Christ Jesus, so we can do the good things he planned for us long ago."*

For many years, I don't think I knew the real me. I was a people pleaser for most of my life, subconsciously becoming who I thought others wanted me to be. But that came at a price. I did not go so far as to be what Julia Roberts depicted in the movie *Runaway Bride*. I at least knew how I liked my eggs cooked, but I was still far from being my authentic self.

Over time, it became exhausting to keep wearing a mask and not truly be who God created me to be. The me that wasn't perfect or happy or confident all the time. The me that wanted to do more for God and be a "difference maker." The me that knew I had gifts to share but felt like I'd be accepted more if I continued to play small. The me that was too scared to illuminate and shine my light.

Natalie Grant's song *The Real Me* perfectly explains how I felt during those years. It's a great song about the masks we wear and the toll that doing so takes on us over time. But thankfully, God knows who we really are and loves us just the same. Thankfully, He is patient in His unconditional love.

Maybe you've been playing small and wearing masks too. Maybe you're reading this book because you're tired of the song and dance, and you're ready to step out and be all that you were created to be. Maybe you know, deep down, that you have something to share, personally or professionally, that could make an impact in someone else's life. Maybe, like me, you're ready to finally shine *through* your story.

It's time for you to illuminate and shine from within! To finally play big and boldly step out of your comfort zone. To create a life that serves God and others.

To assist you along this journey, I've created a simple formula to help you gain clarity on how to illuminate your inner light and share your story for God's glory.

It follows the acronym **S.H.I.N.E.**

> **S** – Sow Your Seeds of Greatness
> **H** – Honor Your Story
> **I** – Identify What's Holding You Back
> **N** – Now is the Time to Write Your Story
> **E** – Encourage and Equip Others

Throughout the rest of this book, we will unpack these concepts together. I will give you suggestions and different exercises that you can do to help you grow in your confidence to share your story. You will also gain a greater understanding of why you have been called for this purpose as we unpack how God is leading your life. And we'll look at ways you can use your story to shine a light for others on the same path. In the end, if nothing else, it is my sincere desire that you will learn a bit more about yourself and God's desires for your life.

ALL THE DIFFERENCE FOR A STARFISH

Now, if you're anything like me, you may still not be convinced that your story matters. After all, you're just one person … how could you really make an impact in this world? Well, that reminds me of the story of the starfish.

One day, an old man was walking along a beach that was littered with thousands of starfish, all of which had been washed ashore by the high tide.

As he walked along, he came upon a young boy who was eagerly throwing the starfish back into the ocean, one by one.

Puzzled, the old man looked at the boy and asked him what he was doing. Without looking up from his task, the boy replied, *"I'm saving these starfish, sir."*

The old man chuckled aloud. *"Son, there are thousands of starfish and only one of you. What difference can you make?"*

The boy picked up a starfish and gently tossed it into the water. Then he turned to the man and said, *"I made a difference for that one!"*

Life has a way of making people cynical. Just like that old man walking on the beach, many people conclude that their lives don't matter. They think that they are unable to make a difference in a large and vast world, populated by so many other people. They see the value in others but are blind to their own value.

> I made a difference for that one!

But the truth of the matter is, all throughout history the course of humanity has been dramatically altered by people willing to make a difference. Innovations have been created, wars have been won, institutions built, and entire nations changed through the power of just one person. Think of Thomas Edison, Mother Teresa, or Moses. After all these years, we remember these people because of their stories.

And while their stories are pretty remarkable, your story doesn't have to be quite as dramatic in order to make a difference. Here's the thing. God doesn't make "average" people, so there's no such thing as an "average" story. It is important to also remember that God does not make mistakes. You are unique, special, and valued in the eyes of the Father. He has given you your story, whatever it is, to shine as a light for others.

You can shine a light for others by sharing your story—your passions, experiences, skills, talents, and knowledge—with those who need to hear it. How amazing would it be to share your story and have the confidence to know that you did make a difference in the world ... again, *even if* it was just for one person?

For you to know that, just perhaps, there was actually a purpose to the pain, to the struggle, or to all the hard lessons you've learned along the way. And for you to know that in all of it, God was preparing you to share your story in order to serve others and create your legacy?

> **He has given you your story, whatever it is, to shine as a light for others.**

Would it be worth it to you then? What if I told you that one could even be a future generation you will never meet? Would you be willing to try and make a difference with your story for just "that one"?

What I hope you realize by reading this book and following the S.H.I.N.E. formula is that you already have everything within you to make a difference, share your story, and serve others *with* your story.

And in doing so, you will **SHINE Through Your Story**.

CHAPTER THREE

BEFORE YOU CAN SHINE OUTWARD, YOU HAVE TO LOOK INWARD

"The purposes of a person's heart are deep waters,
but one who has insight draws them out."
(Proverbs 20:5)

For as long as I can remember, I always wanted to be "the best." I wanted to be the smartest, prettiest, and the most successful. Yet, much of my life, I never really thought I fit my definition of those things. I just possessed a deep, burning desire to be "successful."

I see now that I set myself up for failure, as nothing I did was ever good enough to meet *my* definition of success. It was unreachable because my benchmark kept moving as I moved up the ladder of life.

Reachable or not, my desire to be "the best" made me quite competitive in my high school years. I was determined to be well-liked and involved in as many school activities as I could. I set out to be a leader or an officer in several groups, including becoming captain of the drill team. I'm proud to say my ambition got me most of the things I strived for—but not everything.

My grades were not very good compared to many of my peers. I wasn't the prettiest. I didn't get all the accolades and awards I had hoped to achieve. In fact, the only "award" I got in high school was "Most Friendly." And at the time, I was so disappointed because what I really wanted to be was "Most Beautiful" or "Prom Queen" (a title my best friend won instead).

I know, I know! How shallow was that of me? I wish I could say that I was thankful for getting recognized for *something* when the majority of others did not get a thing, but I had some growing to do back then.

But I was not deterred. I kept after every opportunity to achieve success. I sought leadership titles and tried to remain active in everything I could. It was not all fun and games, though. It was hard, and to say I was stretched too thin is an understatement. It was during those years that I developed a foundation for spreading myself a bit too thin, which carried on for a good part of my life.

Oh, if I only knew back then what I know now. We all say this, but I am a firm believer in that familiar adage of, "Everything happens for a reason." I now know that those challenges and the ones yet to come were there to build me into the person I am today. Without going through the challenges, I could not relate to all the people doing the same today. If I could not relate, I could not help them find their light, which is part of my big purpose.

I'm sure part of what I was trying to do was prove to others that I had what it took. But really, I think deep down I just needed to prove it to myself.

My search for accolades and proving I had what it took did not end with high school. This competitive spirit continued well into college. The pressure was on! I *had* to be a 4.0 student, president of my sorority, and involved in numerous extracurricular activities, including being nominated to Student Government.

I am not trying to say that competitiveness and working towards being the best is bad. What I am trying to say is that it all comes at a cost—both to you and those around you—so you must be sure that it is worth it. You must be doing your best to be the best for the right reasons. You must have balance, or your light may be short-lived.

> You must be doing your best to be the best for the right reasons. You must have balance, or your light may be short-lived.

When I was in college, I had a roommate that loved Amy Grant. I wasn't familiar with her music at the time but after hearing it, I fell in love with the song, *All I have to be*. The words are incredible, and it was such a great reminder for me as I tried so hard to be "the best" in college and life. One of the lines from the song that really resonated with me most was, *"The more I try to be the best the more I get the worst and I realize the good in me is only there because of who you are...All I have to be is what you made me, any more or less would be a step out of your plan..."* If you are struggling with being an over-achiever like me then I encourage you to listen to that song as a reminder that all you have to be is the YOU that God created you to be!

My light was bright, but the cost of it all gave me a little flickering here and there, especially when I veered off track with my purpose or needed a rest. The important thing is to stay in touch with who you are, Whose you are, and stay aligned with your why.

My ambition and drive didn't end in college. In fact, it just intensified as I graduated from college and started my career. Ultimately, I began working for Zig Ziglar, which had been a goal of mine since I was 18 years old (more on that story later).

I did all these things in high school, college, and beyond—but nothing was ever enough. Once I'd tasted greatness within me, I wanted more. But now I also understand that I was looking in the wrong places to make it a reality. I now know that searching for titles is a bit of "superficial" success rather than being an accurate symbol of it. More importantly, I understand that my value was with me throughout my entire journey, as I am a child of God.

Getting Back on Track

I think deep down, we all want to be "the best" at something. We want to be successful or recognized as being good at or accomplishing something. We want to feel good about ourselves and have validation to back it up. But if you're anything like I was, a lot of those successes, accolades, and achievements aren't really based on anything that truly matters in life.

When I think back, I wonder: Why did I want to be captain of my drill team or president of my sorority? I'm very proud of those leadership opportunities, but why did I strive so hard to get them? What was my definition of success at that stage of my life? What's my definition of success now? I'm still trying to figure that out as my journey matures, but I have a much clearer picture of it. My definition of ultimate success is to shine my light as bright as I can so that God gets the glory.

I've matured so much through the years. Yes, my eyesight may not be as good as it used to be, but I see everything in life so much more clearly than I could during those early years. Back then, it was all about *me*, or what people thought of me, and not about Him.

Clarity is the key. Without clarity on what and why we are trying to achieve success, we may be working towards the wrong things for the wrong reasons. It's like this quote I once heard …

"People may spend their whole lives climbing the ladder
of success only to find, once they reach the top, that
the ladder is leaning against the wrong wall."
(Thomas Merton)

Is your ladder leaning against the wrong wall? Do you even know what wall you want it to be on? These are tough questions to answer—or at least they were for me. The easiest way to get clarity is to ask yourself questions like:

… What do I really want for my life?
… What do I want for my family?
… What do I want for my career?
… What do I want for my personal life?
… What do I want to do for God?
… What legacy do I want to leave?
… Why do I want these things?

Those are important questions. Because as we go through this book and I give you the tools to help you shine your light, we have to get clarity on our WHY.

Colossians 3:23 says, *"Whatever you do, work at it with all your heart as working for the Lord, not for human masters."* So, to be successful, we have to work at it. In order to shine our light, we have to put in the effort.

Thinking back to the hard work and effort I put in while working for Zig Ziglar, I can honestly say one of my greatest achievements was winning the coveted title of "Salesperson of the Year." I was so proud of that accomplishment, and I felt Zig and the company were proud of me too. I was given a plaque to celebrate the milestone. I still have this plaque almost 25 years after receiving it.

For those of you wondering about Zig Ziglar, he was America's most influential and beloved motivational speakers. Zig influenced an estimated quarter of a billion individuals through his 33 books, including his bestseller, *See You At The Top*, which has sold almost two million copies. It was an incredible honor to work for Zig and to say he had a big influence in my life is a total understatement!

One of the things I loved most about the awards at Ziglar was that Zig would personally pick a Bible verse for the person receiving the award to be inscribed on the plaque. The special verse Zig chose for me when I was awarded "Salesperson of the Year," was Matthew 6:33 NIV:

> *"But seek first his kingdom and his righteousness, and*
> *all these things will be given to you as well."*

I never really analyzed the Bible verse that Zig picked out for me until recently. We had just moved, and as I pulled the plaque out of a moving box to hang it in my new office, it hit me. After re-reading the verse, it occurred to me that what I was seeking in high school, college, and beyond was my own success. I was seeking to be "the best" for the wrong reasons.

Maybe Zig subconsciously knew he needed to remind me to seek first His kingdom and His righteousness, and then all these things would be given to me. I had it backwards for a really long time—and I'm still working on getting it right now—but I can say for sure that I needed that reminder then, and even now.

> **After you have sought after the Lord and He gives you the desires of your heart, what do you want those desires to be? What is it that you want the Lord to give you? And are you seeking Him first to get those things, or are you trying to figure it out on your own?**

When you think about your own definition of success, I want you to consider it through the lens of what Matthew said in that scripture. After you have sought after the Lord and He gives you the desires of your heart, what do you want those desires to be? What is it that you want the Lord to give you? And are you seeking Him first to get those things, or are you trying to figure it out on your own? Checking in with yourself and God periodically will ensure you are on the right track in your season in life. After all, things change—and sometimes quickly.

If I asked a group of people what their definition of success is, I'd probably get a different response from every single person. I have learned through my many years of coaching and speaking that we all define success differently. Some people define success as recognition, a title, making a certain amount of money, living in a certain size house, or raising a loving, caring family. There are no right or wrong definitions of success. The key is that we understand what it is for us and what we know in our heart as our own truth. So, let me ask you, what is *your* definition of success?

My Definition of Success is…

....

....

....

....

....

....

Through the years, I've had the privilege of meeting some incredibly talented speakers and authors. I'm astounded at the opportunities I've been blessed with and the people I've shared the stage with. One day I started thinking about all these people that I look up to. I was curious as to what makes them all "successful." I mean, what is it really? Why is one person considered successful and the other one isn't?

After much time thinking quietly on it, it became clear to me. What I find consistent across all of them is that they're all passionate about what they do. They're all living life on purpose. They're not second-guessing themselves or the gifts that God has given them to share with the world. Yes, the people I consider as having achieved success seem to have clarity of who they are, why they're here, and what their light is. And they're out there shining that light.

If that's the case, then that means all of us can live on purpose, too, if we take time to gain clarity and then follow our heart. So, let's start there. It is time for us to get clarity!

QUESTIONS TO FIND YOUR PASSION AND PURPOSE

We all have something we are meant to do in this lifetime that supports God's master plan. It's called a purpose. Your passion will be tied to your purpose—because I just know that God isn't going to give you a purpose in life that you hate, right?

You are here for a reason. So, let's uncover it, or at least that next step in your journey to your purpose. And we'll go on this journey together by having you answer a few questions to dive a little deeper.

I want you to write down the answers to these questions on a piece of paper, or in this book—or better yet, in your personal journal for later reflection. The answers to these questions are going to give you insight into your purpose. As I said earlier, before we can shine outward, we must look inward.

Question #1: What Activities Do You Most Enjoy?

....
....
....
....
....
....

Do you love to paint, travel, run? Do you love to be around children, motivate others, write? What are you doing when the time is flying by? And what are you drawn towards when it comes to doing things in your free time? Those are all clues to who you are and why you're here.

Question #2: What Would You Do If You Could Not Fail?

....

....

....

....

....

....

That's a hard question to answer, I know. I want you to really think about this and allow yourself to dream beyond what you might be used to doing today. Take the blinders off and think, "Okay, if I had all the money in the world or all the time in the world, what would I do?" Yes, what would you do if you didn't have a mortgage to pay, or didn't have responsibilities? What would you be doing instead? If you were guaranteed that whatever you started—whether it be a business, a ministry, a book—would be a success, a huge success, what would you want to accomplish? What would you do if you could not, would not, guaranteed will not, fail? Write it down. Remember, God parted the Red Sea. So, anything can happen!

> **What would you do if you could not, would not, guaranteed will not, fail? Write it down.**

Would you start a business? Maybe you'd want to go climb Mount Everest or buy a beach house. Maybe you'd want to quit your corporate job and travel the world. Maybe you'd want to start a family or get married, be a successful author or painter. Really stretch your imagination beyond what you see for yourself today. Don't limit yourself. Write whatever comes to mind.

At one point in my life, I considered what *I would be* if I knew I could do anything with guaranteed success. I wrote that I wanted to be a speaker, author, and coach. I remember meeting somebody one time who gave me their business card, and that was their title. I said, "Oh, wow, someday that's what I want my title to be." I'm incredibly blessed and a bit humbled, but go figure, that is my title now.

So, why am I having you ask that question for yourself? Because in life, we often limit ourselves. We set goals that we know we can achieve, or we think just a little bit outside of our comfort zone instead of doing what we really want to do. Maybe we are fearful that it won't work, or that people won't like it. Or we think "Who am I to do something like that?" We think we are not good enough or that our dreams are for "other" people. Or is it just me thinking those things?

The bottom line is when we can expand our minds to think beyond what we're capable of today, we can get clarity on our purpose. I believe that God gives us dreams and desires that really push our limits (as opposed to comfortable goals that we can easily do on our own). He wants us to know He is there with us every step of the way, giving us special talents and skills to make big things happen in our lives.

> **God gives us dreams and desires that really push our limits (as opposed to comfortable goals that we can easily do on our own).**

I was reminded of that this morning, as I was doing my devotional. The desires of your heart have been planted by a good and loving Father. And even though they may seem so far away right now—so, so far—it's never too late. God is faithful, and if He gave you the desire, then He will bring it to fruition. But many times, we allow doubt in. We limit ourselves to our desires, don't we?

Maybe we think we're not worth our dreams or that we'll never have enough money to do it. Perhaps we think, "I'm just from a small town. Who am I to do anything like this?" Well, that's the whole point of this book. Who are you to NOT do something like this?

Question #3: What Ideas Are You Most Inspired By?

....

....

....

....

....

....

Meaning when you're reading the news or watching TV, what are you drawn to? Is it politics? Is it global warming? Christian values? Leadership? What inspires you? Personal growth? Women's issues?

Think about it this way. When you go to a bookstore, what section do you end up in? That's a big clue. I can learn a lot about a person based on where they are in a bookstore. So, really think about it.

For me, I love personal development, I love leadership. I love all things growth and development. So, that's where you're going to find me in a bookstore. Now, my husband, he's probably going to be in a history section or reading biographies. Some of you I know may end up in the fiction section or the cooking section. Again, there's no right or wrong, but that is a clue to what inspires you.

> When you discover what inspires you, you'll step that much closer to discovering your purpose.

And when you discover what inspires you, you'll step that much closer to discovering your purpose—which, by the way, is your light, which is your story.

I love this next question...

Question #4: When Do You Feel the Most Empowered?

....

....

....

....

....

....

I'll put it another way. When are you most proud of yourself? What are you doing when you know you've done an excellent job? Maybe you never brag about yourself, but inside you know you've "done good," as us Texans would say. Are you leading others? Are you singing? Are you writing? Inspiring others?

If this is a hard question to answer—and for many people it is, especially women—then think about what people compliment you on. Is it your cooking, your hospitality, your unique ability to listen or inspire? When we figure this out, that's when our lights start shining brightest. And as the song said, we're supposed to let it shine. So, what are you doing when your light is shining brightest?

Question #5: What's On Your Bucket List?

....

....

....

....

....

....

There was a movie several years ago called *The Bucket List*. It's a cute movie about these two men who are getting ready to "kick the bucket," so they make a list of all the things they want to do before they die.

We know we're supposed to do this, but have you written out your list? I hadn't until a couple of years ago, which is what really prompted this question: What is it I really want to do before I die?

What is it that you want to do? No matter what, at the end of your life, when you're sitting on your deathbed, what is it that you wish you would have done? Author a book? Start a ministry? Travel the world? Go on a mission trip? What's on your bucket list?

Our final question to help us get clarity on our purpose, is really the most important question:

Question #6: What Legacy Do You Want to Leave?

....

....

....

....

....

....

Obviously, we all know we're going to die someday. Nobody likes to think about it, but we know it's true. So, when you're gone, what do you want people to remember about you? What impression do you want to make during your time here on earth? That's your legacy. Do you want people to remember your accomplishments? Do you want them to remember your smile and your kind spirit? Do you want them to remember how you made them feel?

Remember, if you are reading this book, then you are still living and breathing. That's the beauty of asking yourself this question now—you can still create a life that will leave the legacy you want to leave, starting today! But if we don't think about it now, it will be too late by the time we are ready to leave that legacy. So, what do you want your legacy to be for your loved ones, your business, your community, for God? We all need to start living *now*, while we're still in our living years.

> We all need to start living now, while we're still in our living years.

This book is intended to ignite your light, your spark, so that you can shine. And not only to light other people's paths, but ultimately to glorify God. I love these questions so much! They are the exact questions I asked myself when I was struggling with figuring out my own purpose in years past. I didn't have the answers to these questions immediately, and even now, I continue to revisit them as often as possible.

Once I had gained clarity of my purpose, I also gained motivation to write my book, share my story, and to inspire and motivate others. It wasn't because of me, but because I figured out that I have this ability to share something with others that could change their life and the lives of those around them. And if I have the ability to shine my light and share it with others, then you do too. You have a bright light, a flame within you that is just dying to burst through. You have a purpose, and your life, your story, is a gift from God.

I am most in tune with the deeper parts of myself and my light within when I get away from the noise and spend time in nature. Do your best to do the same. Take a day away. Go somewhere where you find inspiration. Maybe visit a park, pond, or nearby lake. When we take time out of our busy schedules to listen to our inner voice and God speaking to us, we will always get the answers we're searching for. If you don't have the opportunity to get away, take a little extra time in the shower or having your morning coffee before the house starts stirring.

Shining our light isn't for our own purpose—it's for others, and for God. We will enjoy the collateral benefits, though. But how can we know how to do that or what we would say to help others if we don't even know who we are? Take the time now to look inward so that you can shine outward.

If you have any doubts, know that you are worth it. And know that while God is patient, time is of the essence if you want to live out your best life for as long as possible.

> You have a bright light, a flame within you that is just dying to burst through.

I encourage you not to gloss over the questions I've posed. I think discovering your purpose is the key to shining your light, and that's why we're starting here. If you take the time to answer these questions honestly now, and on an annual basis, you'll get the clarity you need to fulfil your God-given purpose.

WHICH ROAD WILL YOU TAKE?

Now that you have a little more clarity regarding your passions and purpose, I want to dive a little deeper into how to make your dreams and goals a reality.

In the late eighties, there was a movie called *Made in Heaven* that I absolutely loved. I'm not really sure why I loved it so much. It's quite cheesy when I watch it now, but still it touched me in such a way. It's about a couple that meets in heaven, and they fall deeply in love. But then they are separated when Annie is sent back to earth to earn her wings. Mike is beside himself with despair. But lucky for him, the heavenly powers offer him a deal. Mike can return to earth, but only on the stipulation that he and Annie will not remember each other. They are given thirty years to find one another.

Back on earth in a physical body, Mike can't seem to get his act together. "There must be something more to life," an inner voice keeps insisting. "There must be a reason I'm here."

The harder Mike tries to ignore that inner voice, the more persistent it becomes. Then one day Mike meets some people who sense that he is struggling to unleash a strong inner desire. It seems to be connected to Mike's love of music, specifically to fragments of a song that keep playing over and over in his head.

To better express this song, Mike teaches himself how to play the saxophone. To his delight, the more skillful he becomes as a saxophone player, the more he can bring forth fragments of the song. Ultimately, it is Mike's magnificent saxophone performance of the song in its entirety that reunites him with Annie.

To this very day, I can still remember the words of Mike's song. Probably because at that point in my life, they struck a chord in me and maybe I needed to hear them.

"If you don't really know where you want to go, it makes no difference which road you take."

> **If you don't really know where you want to go, it makes no difference which road you take.**

How many of us are walking down roads that are leading nowhere? How many of us have a feeling that our lives could be happier and more prosperous, but our current circumstances are holding us back and making it impossible to succeed? The "Mike" from *Made in Heaven* didn't know where he was going, because he didn't know what he wanted. Because he didn't have a purpose, he didn't care where he ended up. Could that Mike (or Mary) be you?

We may be aimlessly scrolling through social media—doing this activity, that activity—with no real thought of why, no real clear direction, no goal. I don't think any of us really want to admit we do that, but the truth is, we all do. We either don't have clarity on what we want, or we know what we want, and we procrastinate on it or doubt ourselves.

I'm not going to dive into procrastination too much now. I actually wrote a whole book on it called *Busy Being Busy...But Getting Nothing Done?*, and I'll touch more on it in Chapter 6. The thing with procrastination is that we're typically not procrastinating on what *doesn't* matter. We usually procrastinate on the things that we know are going to make us happier, healthier, have better relationships, a better career, prosperity, etc.

How many of you, when you woke up this morning, immediately checked your email or spent way too much time scrolling through social media? Did that time bring you closer to your dreams and goals? Or did it move you farther away? You won't get that time back, so it is best not to waste it with excessive "brainless activity." I like a little brainless activity here and there when I am overworked and overstressed, but I cannot live my life absorbed in it. Will the way you spend your first waking hours make your heart's biggest desires come true? If it was spent on social media and email, probably not.

My point is, we find the time to do things that won't lead us where we ultimately want to go. We procrastinate on the things that God has placed in our heart. Or maybe you're not even sure what those dreams and goals are. So, that's what we're going to focus on for just a moment.

I want you to think about your life. Think about it holistically. Zig Ziglar has a tool called *The Wheel of Life* that looks at your life as a whole. He understood that you're more than your career and you're more than your personal or family life. You're more than the money you make or the job that you have, both of which can disappear in an instant. He insists you need to look at yourself holistically, especially when it comes to setting goals. When you clarify the goals that you want to achieve in all areas of your life, and you place them within the spokes of your wheel (Personal, Mental, Career, Financial, Family, Spiritual, and Physical), you'll achieve balanced success.

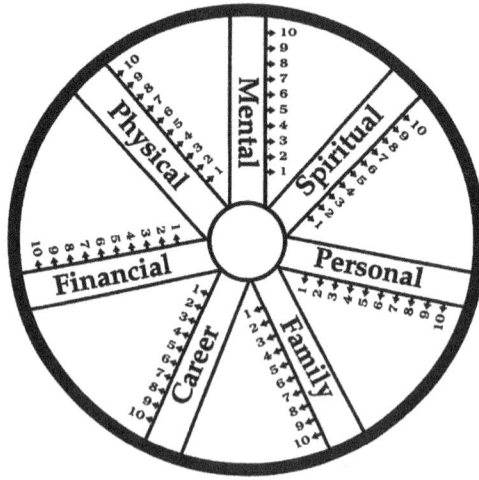

So, let's talk dreams and goals! What do you want for your career? How much money do you want to make? Where do you want to be when you're 65 years old? 75 years old? Where do you want to live? What do you want to accomplish personally and professionally? How do you want to spend your days? Those are all questions to get you closer to what you really want for your life. Goals are critical in staying on track and being accountable for all that you are striving for in life. Go ahead and write down at least one goal in each area of your life:

Personal

....
....
....
....
....
....

Family

....
....
....
....
....
....

Career

....
....
....
....
....
....

Financial

....
....
....
....
....
....

Physical

....
....
....
....
....
....

Mental

....
....
....
....
....
....

Spiritual

....
....
....
....
....
....

So many people go through life asleep. Well, maybe not totally asleep. They're in that comatose state where they're going through life without giving it a lot of thought. Worse yet, the thoughts they do have are defeating. No fingers pointed here. Actually, I'm speaking for myself at times. But you wake up, go to work, pay the bills, take care of the kids, do what you have to do or what we think we *should* do. It is like that movie *Groundhog Day*, where the day starts over every morning and the experiences are all the same. But there are changes we can make in how we approach each day.

> So many people go through life asleep. Well, maybe not totally asleep. They're in that comatose state where they're going through life without giving it a lot of thought.

I hate the word "should." I'm sure I'm not the only one that heard things like, "You should do this, you should do that, you should, should, should, should…" Stop the "shoulds," for goodness' sake! Instead, focus on what you *will do*. What do you want to do? What brings you joy?

LET THE JOURNEY BEGIN

The answers are within you. Getting clarity on that now is important because in order to shine through your story, you must know what and for whom you are called to shine. The foundational part that I'm walking you through of finding your purpose and then getting very clear on your goals—that's what's going to lead you to knowing who you are and what your story is.

It's important to point out that sharing our story isn't about writing a book. It's not about making it about us. It's about sharing what we know, what we've learned, what we've been through with someone else to connect with them, perhaps inspire them, guide them, or even warn them.

I want to encourage you to be open to the idea that you *do* have a story to share. I also want to give you the freedom to know that it's okay if you're not ready to share it just yet. Let's talk about how you could share it when you're ready. You do have a story, and you must trust me when I say: your story matters.

> I want to encourage you to be open to the idea that you do have a story to share. I also want to give you the freedom to know that it's okay if you're not ready to share it yet.

People have said that we should write the story that we need to read. And if we impact just one person, it is worth it. Someone you may know or someone you may have never met is waiting for your story. If nothing else, you can have peace that you are serving God and His people by sharing your testimony. His good works within you, His triumphs over the darkness in your life, and His never-ending faithfulness. As we go through this journey together, I pray that the answers you're seeking become clear and that you see the power in your story.

CHAPTER FOUR

S.H.I.N.E - SOW YOUR SEEDS OF GREATNESS

*You did not choose me, but I chose you and appointed you so that
you might go and bear fruit—fruit that will last—and so that
whatever you ask in my name the Father will give you.*
(John 15:16)

I have a sign on my desk that reads, "You Were Created to Make a Difference!" A good friend of mine gave it to me for my birthday a few years ago, and I love the daily reminder that I, faults, and all, was created to make a difference.

It's not just to make a difference for ourselves, our families, and others (which isn't a bad thing), but it's to make a difference for God. And we can do that by shining our light as an example for others.

It's so simple, yet we tend to make it so complicated. We get in our own way and fool ourselves into thinking that we're not that special or that we don't have much to offer. We may be tied up in our past or our flaws. But doubting ourselves like this only keeps us from sharing our true story, the one God has given us to inspire, motivate, encourage, and build up the people He has placed in our life.

When we don't shine, He can't shine.

You Have Seeds of Greatness Within You

Every time I have a speaking engagement, I start off my talk by sharing one of my favorite quotes by my long-time mentor, Zig Ziglar. The quote is:

> *"Man was designed for accomplishment, engineered for success, and endowed with the seeds of greatness."*

I love this quote. It means that no matter who you are or where you've come from, you have *seeds of greatness* within you! You have something unique and special. You didn't earn those "seeds"—you were born with them.

> **When we don't shine, He can't shine.**

What are we supposed to do with seeds? We're supposed to plant them and nourish them. Give them water and sunshine so they can grow into all they were created to be. I discovered my *seeds of greatness* in 1989.

I was just getting ready to go off to college, and my parents wanted to give me a gift. They told me that this gift was going to "take me places," that it would "totally change my life." Well, in my young adult mind, I assumed they were talking about giving me a car. Boy, was I wrong.

My parents didn't give me a car. Instead, they gave me a ticket to a seminar. But this wasn't just any old seminar; it was a *motivational* seminar. Think back to when you were eighteen years old. Did you want to be motivated?

It was a seminar called *Born to Win*, hosted by Zig Ziglar. Of course, I had never heard of Zig, and I certainly didn't want to spend three whole days with him! I admit that I felt pretty let down when they handed me a conference ticket and *not* the keys to my new ride.

My older brother John was "gifted" with a ticket too, so we reluctantly went to the seminar with very low expectations. The audience wasn't exactly what you would consider our peer group. John and I were the youngest in the room, by decades, but we decided to make the most of it anyhow.

Something changed in me that weekend. I absorbed everything I could from Zig and the other speakers. I found myself taking tons of notes, and to my surprise everything really resonated with me at a deep gut level. I knew that I had found my passion in life— even though I wasn't looking for it.

> Man was designed for accomplishment, engineered for success, and endowed with the seeds of greatness.
> –Zig Ziglar

ENTHUSIASM – GOD WITHIN

At the end of the conference, I lined up to have Zig sign my book. As I got closer to him, my enthusiasm grew. I don't know if you have ever experienced something like this—but as my turn came next in line, I had one of those moments where, in my excitement, I said something to him without really thinking about it. Well, it *was* all I'd been thinking about, but I hadn't actually considered saying it to Zig.

As Zig grabbed my book to sign, I looked at him straight in the eyes and blurted out, "I'm going to work for you one day … you just wait and see!"

I couldn't believe it. I felt embarrassed and exhilarated at the same time. It just came right out of my mouth. In typical Zig fashion, he smiled and was very gracious in his reply. Even though it wasn't exactly what most people would say at "hello," I knew in my heart it would happen.

The following Monday, I went off to college and immediately started going through Sorority Rush (now called Recruitment). I never pictured myself as a "sorority girl." In fact, I was quite against the idea of it while I was in high school. You know how it goes, though—one of my friends talked me into it. Turns out it was one of the best decisions I made. I gained leadership skills, achieved a 4.0 GPA (they make you study!), and built life-long friendships.

But the process of going through Rush was a bit daunting, especially for a people pleaser like me. I wanted everyone to like me, and the thought of being interviewed to see if I made the cut to become their "friend" was overwhelming. I stressed about it for weeks leading up to it. But because my parents had *forced* me to attend Zig's seminar a few days prior, I breezed through Rush with a newfound attitude and, thankfully, no problems at all. Thanks, Mom and Dad!

> **The definition of enthusiasm is "God within."**

At Zig's conference, I heard someone say that the definition of enthusiasm is "God within." I loved that concept; it made total sense to me. I reasoned that when I exhibit enthusiasm, I'm really just shining God's light out from within me. If someone doesn't like the light, then they won't like me. And that's okay! I approached Rush with this same attitude, and the results were amazing.

Each day, right before I'd walk into a sorority house to meet the young ladies, I'd say to myself, "Enthusiasm! Enthusiasm! Enthusiasm! Show them God within!" And that's exactly what I did. I wasn't nervous, I wasn't worried; I was confident because I wasn't walking through those doors alone. Looking back—and especially after knowing the intricate details of what it takes to get into a sorority (grades, connections, and many other things that I did not have)—I'm even more certain that the only reason they picked *me* was because they ultimately picked *Him*!

The next four and a half years at the University of North Texas were some of my best years. And honestly, I forgot all about my meeting with Zig Ziglar as time went by. After graduation, I began looking for a job, but the only job I was able to get right out of college was a sales job selling copiers. This wasn't exactly my dream job because I never wanted to be a "salesperson." But here I was, fresh out of school and selling copiers by cold calling on businesses. Lucky me.

I learned a lot during those six months in copier sales. First, I learned what I never wanted to do again—sales! It was *not* for me. Second, I learned the importance of the environment and the people you surround yourself with day in and day out. To be kind, let's just say this environment left a lot to be desired. I wanted to be around others who possessed "enthusiasm" too. I had no idea that what I sought was right around the corner for me ... literally.

COLD CALLING ON MY DESTINY

To say fate intervened (aka, God) is an understatement. Suddenly, life began to come full circle for me. To my amazement, one day as I was cold calling on businesses to sell copiers in Carrollton, Texas, I walked up to a business park and looked up at the sign that read "The Zig Ziglar Corporation." Well, you could have knocked me over with a feather. It is important to note that this was completely unexpected, as I had switched territories with one of my peers that day to cover her territory. This was only one of many miracles that has led me to where I am today, including writing this book for *you* to read!

Instantly, I thought to myself, "That's right ... I'm supposed to work here!" I ran inside and asked the nice lady behind the desk if this was really where *the* Zig Ziglar worked. She smiled and nodded. I then blurted out, "Do you have any job openings? I'll do anything to work here!"

Well, the funny thing was that she told me the only opening they had available was in sales. Ironic, because after selling copiers for six months, sales was the one thing that I swore I would *never* do again. But this was with Ziglar, and it was the only opportunity they had—and one I was somewhat qualified for. So, I went home and typed up my very first official resume. Let me tell you, this was not the type of resume that would typically get someone a job at Ziglar. Again, my only real experience was a short stint cold calling on companies, trying to sell them copiers!

But they saw my passion shining through, and they decided to give me a chance. I ended up interviewing for the job and pretty much got the offer right there on the spot. I don't say that to brag, but just as a testimony to the power of our mind and God. Deep down I knew that it was "supposed" to happen. I found my new home just like that!

Working for Zig had been a goal in the back of my mind since meeting him. So, when the time came and the opportunity opened for me to interview, my passion and excitement were just as high as they were when I asked Zig to sign my book back in 1989. This was my first foundational evidence that my positive thoughts and being clear about my goals mattered! It was like I had been planning for this all along—although somewhat unknowingly!

Programming Your GPS

That's the funny thing about the mind. It really is so much like a computer—it can't help but follow the commands you give it. When you're clear about your goals and begin to think for yourself about what it is you truly want, then your mind can't help but find ways to bring those goals into being.

> When you're clear about your goals and begin to think for yourself about what it is you truly want, then your mind can't help but find ways to bring those goals into being.

For example, let's say that you and I decide to meet at my office in McKinney, Texas, to discuss your story and explore ways that you can use it for God's glory. You live close enough to drive, so on the day of our meeting you get in your car and program into your navigation system, point A, where you're starting from, and point B, where you want to go, my street address.

As expected, the navigation system takes you exactly to your destination, and we have a great meeting. You may not have known in advance what roads you'd be turning on, but it really didn't matter as long as you got there on time, right?

But what happens if you just program in "McKinney, TX" and not my street address? Would we still get to meet in person? Of course not! You may be close, but you'd just end up driving around and around in circles in the vicinity of my office. You wouldn't know where to find me. And your life is the same.

If you set general goals (*I want to be successful, make more money, buy a new house*) but don't specify exactly what you want (*I want to be promoted to VP, make $10,000 more per month, buy a four-bedroom, two-story house with a pool*), you might get close. But you'll never actually achieve what you really want because you didn't get specific enough and program it into the GPS of your mind. This is why I had you write down your goals in Chapter 2 so you could get more clarity on what you really want.

Now, please don't misunderstand what I'm saying. I didn't have it all figured out in the beginning. I didn't have a grand plan for how to get from point A to point B. But God had a plan for me that was far greater than anything I could ask for or imagine (Ephesians 3:20). A plan so great that I couldn't possibly take any of the credit. See, He opened doors that I didn't know existed, let alone know how to open. God is so good!

TRADING IN MY PASSION FOR A BIGGER PAYCHECK

I worked in the Ziglar corporate office for just under four years. Then I decided to do something radical. I decided to quit. I know, what was I thinking, right? Here I had my dream job, and I was walking away from it.

It was one of those times when even though I loved working with Zig, and I loved what I was doing, I had the opportunity to leave my passion for a shot at making more money.

I was in my early twenties then and had a shortsighted view of things. The "dot.com" boom had taken off, and this was my opportunity to make it big.

I was torn between following my passion and following the money. Well, as a young twenty-something, unsurprisingly, I chose the money. And really, I am thankful for that detour. Without it, I may not be doing what I'm doing today, and I likely wouldn't be sharing my story with you in this book.

So, just like that, I entered "Corporate America" and began my career in technology, spending the next thirteen years selling software. At first, it was all so exciting: the hustle and bustle of traveling and doing presentations and software demos for large companies. But that excitement quickly faded.

One thing was for sure: the culture and values in this chapter of my career were vastly different from my days at Ziglar. The thought, taken from a line out of one of my favorite movies, echoed through my mind: "Toto, I have a feeling we're not in Kansas anymore." And boy, was that right!

Those thirteen years taught me lessons that I couldn't have learned had I stayed at Ziglar. You see, the farther I was from my passion, the harder it was for me to be truly happy. Even though I was very "successful," I was miserable and unfulfilled on the inside. Here I was doing a job that I *could* do well, but which I didn't love—and it was taking a toll on me.

I was frustrated and discouraged. From the outside, it looked like I had it all together. But on the inside, I was a wreck. I didn't feel fulfilled. Deep inside myself, I knew there was more that I was supposed to be doing. I knew I was supposed to be living my purpose and shining my light, but instead I felt aimless, like I was walking in circles. I didn't know where to turn or who to follow. At that time in my life, I had no idea that I'd been "chosen."

THE CHOSEN

I've been watching a great new series called *The Chosen,* by American filmmaker and director, Dallas Jenkins. If you haven't seen it yet, then you must stop what you're doing (well, maybe after you finish this book) and watch it. It will change your life. I don't want to spoil it for you, but it's a drama series based on the life of Jesus of Nazareth told from the perspective of His disciples. It's so good!

What I love about the show is how the disciples seem so real and imperfect. It's refreshing to watch how Jesus chose each and every one of them, even the ones who made major mistakes or lived ungodly lives. He chose them even though they were not the people you'd think the Lord of Lords would surround Himself with during His short time on earth.

> **If He chose us, then certainly He will give us what we need to illuminate His light and love through us.**

Many of these disciples probably thought they chose Jesus because they were ready to serve God and do something good with their lives. But ultimately, Jesus chose them first, and it's the same with us. We are His chosen people, created to live a life of serving others and glorifying God. If He chose us, then certainly He will give us what we need to illuminate His light and love through us. All we have to do is take inspired action.

STEPPING OUT IN FAITH

I have always had this feeling deep inside that I wanted to make a big difference in the world. I wanted to help people and inspire others, just like Zig had done. I prayed so hard for God to use me. I told Him

I was ready. Then, I impatiently kept problem-solving in my mind to find answers on how to do it myself.

Every time I thought about my story, my passions, or considered what it was that I believed I was made for, I kept coming back to the same three words: **motivate**, **inspire**, and **encourage**. But I had no idea *how* to do it. So, I went back to do what I could control—I prayed for answers … a lot! I kept asking God to show me *how* to make a difference and ignite my light from within for His glory. It didn't happen overnight, but eventually I heard Him speak directly to me. It wasn't an audible voice, per se, but I felt it in my heart and gut. I took out my journal and began to write what I heard.

Journaling has always been a big part of my life, and it's one of the ways I best communicate with God. So, as I journaled, it became clear what God was telling me to do.

It was 2008, and in my prayer time, I very clearly heard God say to me, *"Write!"* Now, some of you may be thinking that's crazy. But the truth is that God does speak to us—*if we listen*. This was not a "still, quiet voice." It was a loud and clear directive: *"Michelle … Write!"*

Of course, I was stubborn and didn't really believe He was telling me to *Write*. Surely He was saying *Right*, as in right or wrong, or something like that. But in my soul, I knew what it meant. He wanted me to write a book.

> **I humbly said to God, "But I have nothing to say!" And I believed it.**

Still unwilling to accept the assignment, I humbly said to God, *"But I have nothing to say!"* And I believed it. I'm embarrassed to say so now, but that encounter with God went on for two years. Yes, two whole years! That's how stubborn I was—or am, actually! I just couldn't fathom how God could use someone like *me*, because I didn't feel I had anything to offer … or anything that people would care about.

I was also still so wrapped up in being a people pleaser that my first thought was, *"What will all my friends and family think?"* Looking back now, I can see how foolish those thoughts were. But they were very real to me at the time. Deep down I knew that if I wanted to make a difference, I had to share my story beyond my journal—but my doubts and fears were stopping me in my tracks. The only thing pushing me forward was knowing that God was telling me to do it, and I didn't want to disobey Him.

So, I convinced myself to write my book. I reasoned that I'd probably just share it with my husband and our boys, anyway. If nothing else, I thought it would be a nice legacy to leave for my family. And since I was doing the book "for them," I could press forward with writing it. I knew they would love me, no matter how good or bad it turned out to be.

> **Deep down I knew that if I wanted to make a difference, I had to share my story beyond my journal.**

When Inspiration Hit

Finding the time to write a book while raising two boys in elementary school, traveling all over the country selling software, volunteering at church, and making time to be a good wife, daughter, and friend was all a bit more challenging than I thought it would be. I had plenty of valid excuses that could tie up my progress for years, but God was ignoring my plea! He knew I could do it, despite how busy I told Him I was at the time.

I remember one Saturday morning, I felt inspired to write a chapter. So, I asked my husband, Chris to take the kids to the park, to the store, or anywhere so long as they got out of the house. Since the kids were still little, they would follow me around the house, asking all kinds of precious questions. But I knew I had to get this—whatever *this* was—out of my head and onto paper. I needed my wonderful little "distractions" to go away, at least for the next hour.

Once they left and I started to write, I wrote so quickly that I didn't even remember what I had written. I had to go back and reread the chapter. And to my surprise, it wasn't bad! When Chris came home with the boys, I sheepishly asked him to read it. He went into the bedroom and took what seemed like an eternity. Then he came out, gave me a huge hug, and said, *"I'm so proud of you! This is so good! I totally get it now."*

> **That's when the doors of opportunity that I never could have imagined flew open for me.**

Amazingly, I wrote the book in just a few short weeks. And that's when the doors of opportunity that I never could have imagined flew open for me.

Once the first draft was in the editing phase, I started to work on the book cover. I really had no idea what I wanted for the cover, so when the book designer asked me if I was putting my picture on the front, a resounding *"No!"* came out of my mouth. That felt too bold for me, as I didn't want to put myself out there *that* much. I wanted to stay under the radar with it. I hadn't told anyone about the book, except for my parents, husband, and kids. So, I certainly wasn't going to put my face on the cover!

I had thoughts like, *"Who do you think you are, Zig Ziglar or something?"* Those kinds of limiting beliefs and self-doubts kept running through my mind. And, because we were in a tight financial situation at the time, and because this was considered a "passion project" of mine, I didn't feel our budget could support getting a professional in-studio photo shoot. The conversation with the book designer was put to bed pretty quickly, never to be considered again … or so I thought.

DIVINE PROVISION

A few hours later, I was waiting in the schoolyard to pick up my younger son from kindergarten, when an acquaintance approached me. Her name is Jennifer, and while we knew each other, we weren't close friends yet.

She said, *"This is going to sound really crazy, but I just started taking a photography class, and my final exam is to do an in-studio photo session. I need a model. Would you be my model?"*

WOW! I literally laughed out loud, looked up at the sky with a big smile, and then graciously said to her, *"Sure. Funny, it looks like I'm 'supposed' to get a professional headshot anyway."* That was my sign.

So, we met at the college, took a few shots, and she snapped the photo that ended up on my book cover—and ultimately all over the media. God is so good!

A few weeks later, I went to lunch with some of my "Ziglar friends." I was sitting next to Laurie Magers, Zig Ziglar's longtime assistant. Laurie is such a loving, kind soul, and I felt safe sharing my book "secret" with her. She asked how I was doing and what was new, so I told her that I had written a book. To which she instantly said, *"Well, you're going to ask Mr. Ziglar to write the foreword, aren't you?"*

I said, *"No! I would never want to take advantage of him or my connection to Ziglar. So, thank you, but no. Plus, I'm not sure it's even any good, and I may not publish it anyway."*

She said, *"Well, Mr. Ziglar won't write a foreword for a book he doesn't like, so you have nothing to lose."* I hesitantly sent it to Laurie and held my breath.

I adored Zig and respected him very much; I never wanted him to feel like I was "using" him to elevate myself. But I can see now how that was my old, low self-esteem rearing its ugly head again. Waiting on his opinion of my work created even more anxiety, but to my surprise, not only did Zig agree to write the foreword, but he wrote an amazing testimonial that means the world to me still today!

This was the confirmation I needed. I was on cloud nine! Having *the* Zig Ziglar write the foreword to *my* book … my little book … was beyond my wildest dreams.

I couldn't believe the favor and grace that had been given to me so freely. The doors of opportunity were opening before my eyes, and I wasn't doing anything to make it happen. It was all God! He was fulfilling the promise I had held on to for all those years while I was yearning to follow my passion and make a difference. He was fulfilling His plans to prosper me and not harm me, but to give me a future and a hope (see Jeremiah 29:11). Once I did as He asked, everything else fell into place.

> **The doors of opportunity were opening before my eyes, and I wasn't doing anything to make it happen. It was all God!**

But it didn't happen overnight; there were plenty of days when I couldn't see the forest through the trees. I'd have moments of ultimate clarity and connection with God—those "mountaintop" experiences—followed by days or weeks of being in the valley with no idea as to where my future was headed. As time passed, I even doubted that I had heard God telling me to "write" many times. But He'd always give me a sign so that I never truly lost all hope. I even told myself that although I have this one good book in me, that does not make me a writer. Oh, how I would deceive myself some days. In the end, I leaned upon God's word and wrote my heart out!

Do You Want a Cup of Coffee?

One day, while I was on my lunch break from my software job, I felt led to go to Mardel's, a Christian bookstore. I had never been there before, so I wasn't sure why I was going, but figured maybe I'd get a little bit of much-needed positivity and inspiration. I walked in and there it was—the coffee mug that changed my life. Sound dramatic? Yeah, it probably was, but it was my sign that God had me in the palm of His hand.

I had been in tears that day for some reason, but this mug, the first thing I saw when I walked in the store, called out to me. God knew I loved coffee, and He found a way to wake me up that day. Jeremiah

29:11 was inscribed on one side of the mug, "'For I know the plans I have for you,' declares the Lord, 'plans to prosper you and not to harm you, to give you a future and a hope.'" The other side of the mug simply read, "Journey." This mug gave me hope and sanity in those dark valley days. I was on my journey… to His greatness.

I clung to that verse in the following days, months, and years. I still do today. And each time I have my coffee, I'm reminded that God has a good plan for me, and I just need to be patient and wait. He is going before me to pave my path. Just like waiting for my coffee, I can wait for my blessings from God … and all the goodness He has for my life. I still have that mug; I always will because it's a reminder of God's faithfulness and unending love for me. I mean, who else would use a coffee mug to change your life but a good and loving Father who knows how much His daughter loves coffee?

A Decision to Follow My Passion

Even as things were starting to really take off with my book, I was still working a full-time software sales job and juggling all the responsibilities of being a wife and mother.

I was busy, but the fire inside of me became so much stronger, and I loved every minute of it. I was full of passion, tenacity, and determination to make it happen. For the first time in my life, I knew exactly what I was meant to do and the why behind it. I was super-charged! I read everything I could find about publishing, building a business, marketing, and public speaking. I attended every conference, mastermind, and program I could that would help me reach the "next level."

It was exciting to see the seeds of my experiences with Zig and the people I worked with at Ziglar starting to sprout in my life. Oh, if I had only known how the time with Zig was shaping me for today! Nothing could stop me back then—I was on my mission! My passion was in overdrive! Yes, it was an exciting time in my life … but also an exhausting one.

Around this time, my husband was starting a new business too, and the more I tried to grow my business, the more I knew I needed to let him build his first. Not to say mine was not as important and growing, because it was … all by referral and the grace of God. But with my growth, I started to hate my software job even more. I longed to break free from the corporate chains and the dangling "golden carrots" of a highly-paid commission role. It was a tough decision to make: *Should I follow the money or follow my passion?*

> **My passion was in overdrive! Yes, it was an exciting time in my life... but also an exhausting one.**

I had to make a similar decision back in 1997 when I decided to stop working for Zig Ziglar and enter software sales. As you remember, following the money of software sales left me unfulfilled. Even though I made the decision to follow the money then, this time I knew I needed to make the decision to follow my passion. Ironically, I had discovered my *seeds of greatness* in 1989, but it wasn't until 2008, almost twenty years later, that I actually did something with them. I finally watered and nourished those seeds, which eventually took root and gave fruit to my first book, *Winning In Life Now*. Fortunately, my family and I were on the same page. They supported my path. I know God was lighting the path for all of us to follow… in sync!

Unique Dreams

Stepping back, a couple of years prior to my "aha" moment to write my first book, I went to a *Women of Faith* conference with an old college roommate. It was an incredible event full of amazing speakers, and it happened to be in Dallas, TX, near where we lived. As we sat in the American Airlines Center, surrounded by 20,000 or so other faithful women, I remember feeling so inspired and happy. I was in my element, and I soaked it up like a sponge.

I leaned over to my friend and, with excitement in my voice, asked, "Wouldn't you love to be a speaker at this event?" I mean, who wouldn't want to be in the spotlight in front of thousands of other people and speak from the heart? Well, clearly not my friend! The look on her face was one of sheer terror. She said, "You couldn't pay me a million dollars to walk out on that stage, let alone open my mouth!"

> **Maybe I did have seeds of greatness that were unique to me. And maybe, just maybe, they were worth exploring.**

It was in that moment I realized that maybe I did have some gifts, talents, and desires that were not like everyone else's. Maybe I did have seeds of greatness that were unique to me. And maybe, just maybe, they were worth exploring. They were for me, and I have a hunch they will be for you too.

So, what about you? What do you think your God-given seeds of greatness are?

My Seeds of Greatness are ...

....

....

....

....

....

....

....

....

Chapter Five

S.H.I.N.E - Honor Your Story

"And we know that in all things God works for the good of those who love him, who have been called according to his purpose."
(Romans 8:28)

I t took me three weeks to write my first book, *Winning in Life Now*, and another seven months to figure out how to publish it. When it was finally complete, it was one of the proudest moments of my life.

I still remember so vividly when I opened my first box of books on St. Patrick's Day, 2009. I cried a cry that I didn't know I had in me. I was so proud of myself for what I had achieved. That feeling of holding my new "baby" in my arms for the very first time was so special, and I was grateful that God had honored me by putting the words in my heart. I was especially grateful that I had finally listened and obeyed His command.

Little did I know that this one act of obedience would lead to the privilege of helping others to tell their stories too. The consistent message I hear from those that I've helped is, "I wish I did this sooner!" Meaning, no one has ever regretted sharing their story ... they only wish they'd acted sooner.

No matter when it happens, it's something that no one can take away from you. It will live on far past your last breath. It is scary, yes, but also exhilarating at the same time.

Believe it or not, even after I had published a book with a foreword written by Zig Ziglar, I still didn't tell anyone. I may have told a best friend or two, but that's it. I was still struggling with my confidence and worried about what other people might think. It wasn't a good place for me to be, but that all changed one afternoon when I attended a SUCCESS event in Dallas.

A Challenge and an Encouragement

I love personal development, so going to events like the SUCCESS event is in my DNA. One of the speakers at the event, let's just call her "Meg" for privacy's sake (you will understand later), made a big impact on me.

I didn't know who she was at the time, but she talked about dreams … *big* dreams. She said we all have dreams, and we never dare to tell anyone our most important ones. So, she challenged us to write down our BIG dream—*the* dream that we had never told anyone.

Well, for the very first time, I wrote, "*I want to be the female version of Zig Ziglar.*" Wow! That was hard to write, and instantly that negative voice came back. "*Who do you think you are? That is not even possible.*" Being the rule follower that I am, I followed Meg's instructions and wrote it down anyway.

After the event was over, I wanted to thank Meg for the challenge she gave us. It really moved me. I said hello, and she asked me to tell her more about myself. At this point, lots of other people were starting to congregate around her to talk to her too, and I didn't want anyone to hear what I said. So, in a whisper, I said, "*I'm in software sales, I have two kids … oh, and I wrote a book.*"

In a very loud voice, so everyone could hear, she said, *"You wrote a book?"*

I smiled and said, *"Yes, and Zig Ziglar wrote the foreword, but I haven't told another soul outside of my family and closest friends."*

At this, she was shocked. As loudly as she could, she shouted into the crowd, *"Listen to this … this woman has written a book endorsed by none other than Zig Ziglar! And she hasn't told anyone!!!!"*

I was mortified.

She added, *"Michelle, let me ask you a question. Do you want to help people? Do you really want to make a difference?"*

I said, *"Of course I do."*

> **You can't make a difference if you don't tell your story.**

"Well, you can't make a difference if you don't tell your story. So, that's what you're going to do. You are going to go home, get on Facebook, and let the whole world know that you've written a book."

I was inspired, challenged, embarrassed, and a little ticked off all at the same time. She then made me an offer I couldn't believe. She said, *"I have a national radio show, and I'm going to have my producer call you on Monday morning to see if you did it. And if you did, I'm going to have you come on as a guest on my radio show."*

At the time, I had no idea how big "Meg" was, and I knew nothing about her radio show. In fact, I was less impressed about her radio show and more terrified at the thought of letting people know I had written a book. But I went ahead and did it anyway.

That night, I went home and made the social media post. *"If anyone is wondering what I've been up to the last few months, I've been writing a book. And if you want to buy it, let me know."*

Orders came flying in from friends, family members, and even strangers! I couldn't believe it, but I was so excited!

Not Quite What I Had Expected

When Monday morning came and the producer called, I proudly told him that yes, I did make my post on Facebook. So, he booked me on the show. I was thrilled beyond belief, but also pretty nervous.

I told all my friends and family to tune in for the interview. I couldn't wait for Meg to praise me over the radio waves for my bravery. But when the radio show started, to my shock, Meg focused instead on my lack of confidence and how she couldn't believe I wouldn't tell anyone about writing a book … *especially* a book with Zig Ziglar's endorsement.

My heart sank, and I was embarrassed because I had told so many people to tune in and listen. But mostly, I was mad! How dare she call me out and make me feel even less about myself than I already felt … and to do it *live on air!* I was crushed.

> **From that moment on, I have never looked back at telling people about my book, my business, and my mission.**

But not for long.

In the end, it all turned out to be a blessing in disguise. It lit a fire in me to show her. I put together a plan to officially launch my book, and before I knew it, I was a "best-selling author." From that moment on, I have never looked back at telling people about my book, my business, and my mission. So, thank you, "Meg!"

A BLUR OF BLESSINGS AND OPPORTUNITIES

Suddenly, my book opened up an entire business of writing, speaking, coaching, and hosting my own seminars—all because I was an author. It didn't happen overnight, but eventually I was able to say goodbye to the corporate job I hated and hello to running my own business, which I did full-time from the comfort of my own home. The sacrifices finally paid off, and I was given the gift of spending more time with my family.

I'm sharing all this with you so that you understand the power of your story. See, I was the exact same person the day before I wrote my book as I was the day after. Only now all these opportunities were coming to me that wouldn't have been possible had I not taken the first step and responded to God's nudges to write a book.

> I was the exact same person the day before I wrote my book as I was the day after. Only now all these opportunities were coming to me that wouldn't have been possible had I not taken the first step and responded to God's nudges to write a book.

After sharing my story in that first book, I've since authored several more books. I have created numerous coaching programs, products, podcasts, and courses, and I get to host regular conferences that I am deeply passionate about. God has helped me design all of this in order for me to help others step into their greatness as well. All because I decided to honor my story!

UNEXPECTED DETOUR

"Be careful what you wish for, because you may just get it." Ever heard that saying? Well, that is exactly how I felt as I was plowing down the pathway of success in my new business. I wanted *so* badly to speak all over the world, to have an incredible coaching and mastermind

business, and to help other people become authors too. And all of that came true—which I'm so incredibly grateful for.

Everything happened so fast, and my path took a different direction for a year or two that didn't look quite like the path I'd started on or envisioned. I was getting lost in the excitement of it all—and fast. During this time, my priorities became blurred, family life became more hectic, and my overall stress increased. After all this running around and flurry of activity, I needed to pause and reevaluate what was most important to me. I had found myself doing everything I *could* to build the business in my own strength, but I hadn't consulted with God first. It was a dangerous situation to be in, and I knew it had to change.

PRIORITIZING THE RIGHT PEOPLE

The world of speaking and traveling to present at various conferences is an interesting one. It's exciting and enticing. Everything was bigger than life, especially to a newbie like me. The allure of fame can really pull you in if you're not careful. It's tempting to think that you really can have it all. And for many on the speaking circuit, that's exactly what they want. *But at what cost?* It's like the Bible verse where Jesus says, *"What good is it for someone to gain the whole world, yet forfeit their soul?"* (Mark 8:36)

Riches and fame in this life don't go far when compared to the endless bounty of Heaven. What good is it if I prioritize my business at the expense of those I love—including myself? None. In fact, I would actually be tearing down the bridges of connection with my family rather than building them up with my business. This was the exact antithesis of what I set out to do with my company and what I believe God nudged me to do in the first place.

I found myself doing things, making business decisions, and associating myself with people that were not in my best interest, just so I would be *perceived* as being "more successful." Thankfully, God stopped me in my tracks and made me realize why I was called to

"WRITE" in the first place. It wasn't to make a certain amount of money, nor was it to feed my ego and selfish desires.

> **The reason God told me to begin writing was to make a difference in the lives of other people – to use this platform for His purposes, not my own.**

The reason God told me to begin writing was to make a difference in the lives of other people—to use this platform for His purposes, not my own. I wanted to make an impact with my business and change lives. And not just other people's lives, those off someplace at a conference or event, but the very people living right under my own roof.

ESCAPING FROM THE PRISON OF REGRET

I'm blessed with a wonderful family, and I would say that I'm a pretty good mom (most of the time). But because I was traveling so much during those couple of years in my business, I unfortunately missed out on many of the "little things" that meant so much in my kids' lives. And that is definitely something I regret. I know the travel had a positive impact on those outside of my family, so it was not a complete waste. But it was not worth it to me when I looked at the toll it was taking on those I loved the most.

I sometimes regretted choosing to speak for a group of strangers instead of reading books to my boys at night. I regretted rushing bedtime and school drop off so that I could get back to work. I regretted passing up girlfriend time because I was "too busy." I regretted not spending enough time with my husband, parents, and extended family. Heck, I regretted not getting more time with myself during this crazy career building season—not to mention pausing for enough quality time with God.

I used to regret so much, but I've come to realize that regret is a trap, like a prison. And the enemy will try to convince you that those negative feelings are true. He wants to keep you focused on the past and what you did wrong, instead of living life forward and stepping into all that God is calling you to. He thrives on stalling our progress. He knows God will get us back on track, but he revels in delays in the meantime.

It was during this most challenging time that I learned that you can't live life looking backwards. The past stays in the past. You can't change it, but you can change your beliefs and behaviors so that you have a better future and, more importantly, a better NOW! Luke 9:62 NASB says, *"But Jesus said to him, 'No one, after putting his hand to the plow and looking back, is fit for the kingdom of God.'"*

> I used to regret so much, but I've come to realize that regret is a trap, like a prison. And the enemy will try to convince you that those negative feelings are true.

Looking back in regret focuses your attention on the wrong that was done. It focuses your energy on the negative, the pain, or the sin, instead of looking to God for forgiveness and healing. So, you must learn to forgive yourself for any of your past regrets. You must commit to a better future. You must move forward and learn the lessons those particular seasons brought. We have enough limits in life, so let's not create more for ourselves.

"STOP!"

I'm certain I learned that lesson loud and clear. I knew from that season on it was to be a new beginning of many positive changes for me. In fact, one very late night during that period, while I was at a conference in Los Angeles, I felt God speak to me again. This time, He said, "Stop!" I was confused … stop what? Stop the business? Stop speaking? Stop following my dream? I now know that He was telling me to stop trying so hard, and to stop chasing the wind. Wow!

When King Solomon wrote Ecclesiastes, he was reflecting on the meaninglessness that his empire had produced. Sure, he had great wealth, fame, and adoration, but his heart was empty. Ecclesiastes 2:10-11 NLT says this:

> "Anything I wanted, I would take. I denied myself no pleasure. I even found great pleasure in hard work, a reward for all my labors. But as I looked at everything I had worked so hard to accomplish, it was all so meaningless—like chasing the wind. There was nothing really worthwhile anywhere."

Rather than feeling fulfilled, King Solomon felt the void of achievement, grace, and significance. He had lost sight of the purpose for his wealth and begun to value his accomplishments and accumulation more than the One who had given it all to him to begin with.

> **God always has a plan for us, and we don't have to strive to make it work...it just will.**

God always has a plan for us, and we don't have to strive to *make it* work … it just will. Here I was, trying to make something happen that really wasn't what needed to happen in that moment. But when I heard God speak this time, I listened to Him right away. I immediately booked a flight home at 5:00 a.m. the next morning, and I left the conference early—a conference that I had paid $2,000 to attend! I knew it was the right thing to do. It was what I *needed* and what I truly was supposed to do. God was giving me one of those little nudges, and I trusted Him. He has never led me astray. Yes, I get confused and offtrack from time to time, but He stays consistent with me until I get it done!

God always has our best interests at heart. And when we obey Him, He rewards us with more intimacy, clarity, and favor. We just have to ask, listen, and be patient with our faith!

Slowing Down to Speed Up

From that point on, I pretty much stopped attending conferences, unless I was the one speaking. I stopped getting coached by other experts, and instead relied on the very best expert of all—God Almighty! I stopped traveling unless it was absolutely necessary, and this was before COVID. And I stopped feeling like I *had* to make this or that happen. All of this "stopping" really allowed my business to gain more momentum.

You see, I figured that if it was meant to be, God would make it happen for me. And what a wonderful blessing it was! I'm not saying going to conferences or participating in coaching programs are bad things or that they're not important. They can be immensely helpful in the right season. And they can do much to build you up as a person and business leader, thus giving you new perspective. But again, it all must take place within God's timing and according to His word.

Again, King Solomon says,

> *"For everything there is a season,*
> *a time for every activity under heaven.*
> *A time to be born and a time to die.*
> *A time to plant and a time to harvest.*
> *A time to kill and a time to heal.*
> *A time to tear down and a time to build up.*
> *A time to cry and a time to laugh.*
> *A time to grieve and a time to dance.*
> *A time to scatter stones and a time to gather stones.*
> *A time to embrace and a time to turn away.*
> *A time to search and a time to quit searching.*
> *A time to keep and a time to throw away.*
> *A time to tear and a time to mend.*
> *A time to be quiet and a time to speak.*
> *A time to love and a time to hate.*
> *A time for war and a time for peace."*
>
> (Ecclesiastes 3:1-8 NLT)

Ironically, even though I stopped all the craziness and extra activities, my business actually exploded. People and opportunities began coming to me, instead of me trying to chase after them. Suddenly, I was invited to be a guest on Sirius XM Joel Osteen Radio and to speak at large churches, like Lakewood. I became an ambassador for Ziglar, Inc., and appeared on numerous TV and other media outlets all over the country. God sped my business up. It was as if I had to make room for it. Take note of this lesson. What is God asking you to make room for in your life?

When I slowed down and stopped trying to do everything, *everything that mattered* started to work out. I prayed more. I spent more time with my family, and we went on more vacations. I released my cares and burdens to the Lord since He's really the only One that can truly handle them anyway. Everything was coming freely to me, but without cost to my family. I had balance, true balance—finally!

> **When we pause to listen for His instruction, God will always provide us with the answers we seek.**

When we pause to listen for His instruction, God will always provide us with the answers we seek. It's a lesson I've had to learn many times over in my life. But now, I pray that I have finely tuned-in "spiritual hearing aids" for the rest of my life. I don't want to miss a single word He says moving forward. Do you?

Right now, take a few minutes and consider, what is God telling you to do? Write down what you hear.

....
....
....
....
....
....

BOOK BOUND

Though I made lots of mistakes in the early years of my business (including racking up over $80K in debt in the first two years), I did do one thing right: I took action ... massive action.

One of the best decisions I made was embracing the opportunity to help others share their stories. Let me be clear: I never set out to do this, nor had I ever wanted to do this in the past. But I saw that many were struggling in this area, and since I just went through it with my book, I knew I could help them. It was natural to me.

In 2010, I borrowed my dad's conference room and invited a small group of people to join me for my first ever *Book Bound* workshop. What started as a one-day seminar with twelve people grew into a three-day book writing, publishing, and marketing "experience" that has spanned over a decade, helping thousands become published authors.

Book Bound is designed to help soon-to-be authors get their story out of their head and onto paper, navigate the publishing process, and learn how to build an author platform so they can make a difference in the world by sharing their story.

I love *Book Bound*; it's my baby. There, I'm in my element, and I feel like my light shines brightest. I say it's not about a book; it's about your story. What I see take place in this event is real transformation. When someone decides to write a book, the experience can be healing. It can provide clarity and an opportunity to meet other like-minded people. Many attendees see, maybe for the first time, who they are and what they have to offer. They see their gifts. More importantly, they find out they are not alone in the questions and struggles of life. They discover how to shine their light, even those that don't know where that light comes from. They find hope and experience validation!

> It's not about a book; it's about your story.

The experience lights a spark for believers and non-believers alike. It's not a faith-based event, per se, but the Holy Spirit is always present, and I can literally see hearts change right before my eyes. Not because of me. It's *Him* working through me, enabling me to illuminate His light and love onto others. I'm so blessed to be used in this way.

On the first day of the workshop, we focus on helping the attendees "find their story." We do this through several exercises to get to the heart of their *seeds of greatness*, and to identify what they could share with others to make a difference.

Now, if you're thinking that you don't want to write a book, that's totally okay! However, I've learned that when you take your story, the combination of your passions and your experiences, and you put them into a book, that's when you have the greatest opportunity to serve more people. As I mentioned, some people write so their own family can hear the full story from their point of view, or so their words can be passed down. Others write for themselves … for their own healing and remembrance. And others write to build their authority and brand. There are all sorts of reasons people put pen to paper. Whatever your purpose, follow the call to action that brought you here. You won't regret It!

> There are all sorts of reasons people put pen to paper. Whatever your purpose, follow the call to action that brought you here.

Ultimately, it's not about the *book*. It's about your *story*.

FINDING YOUR STORY

One of the key exercises we do at *Book Bound* is the Passion/ Experience exercise. This simple method enables people to clearly identify their story by reflecting on their *passions* and *experiences*. It's a powerful exercise, and I've seen the light bulb come on for so many during this part of the workshop. I want to help you do this same exercise so you can get clarity on your story. Many come in with a head full of ideas, and then this exercise clears the clutter. This is one of the most powerful exercises that you can do. Let me show you.

Grab a blank sheet of paper and draw a big T-chart on it. Or use the diagram below.

Passion & Experience Exercise

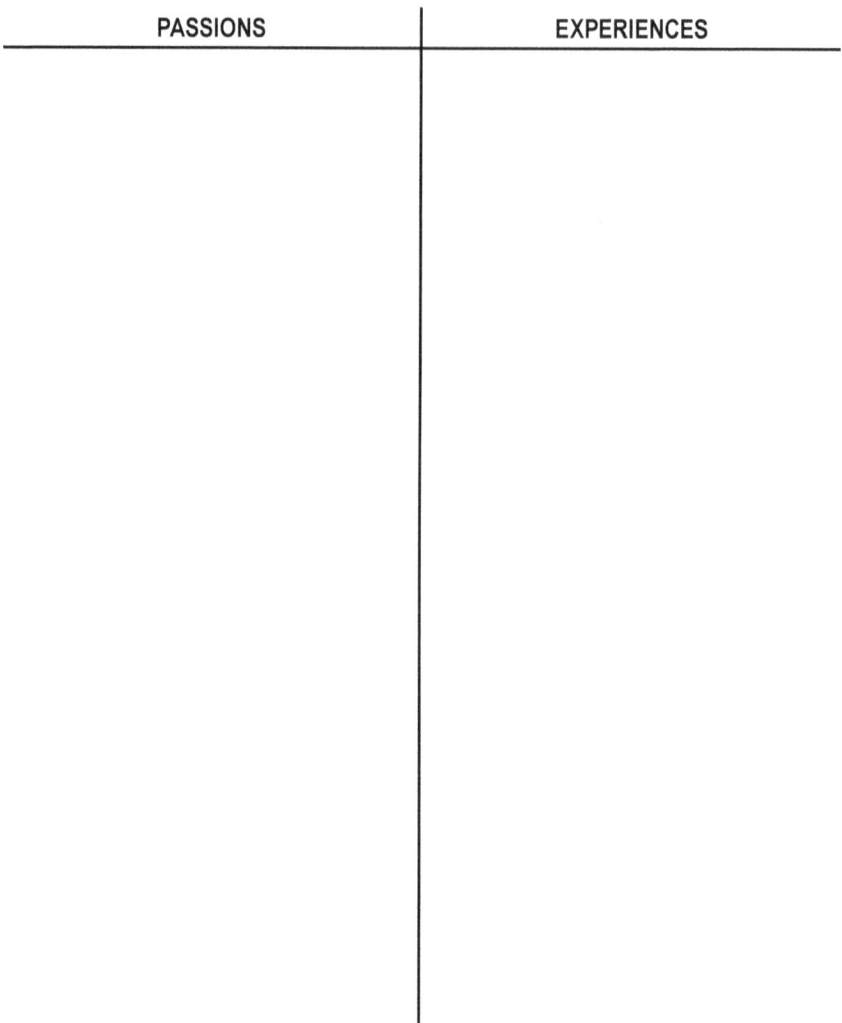

PASSIONS	EXPERIENCES

On the left side of the T, write the word "Passions." Below that, list as many things you can think of that you are passionate about: things you enjoy doing, things that light you up. You can go back to the list of passions that you wrote in the first section of the book or dig a little deeper and add a few more. If you search, you'll see you have lots of passions!

Think about what you're doing when the time passes by so quickly, or you feel like you're in "your own skin." Write down everything that comes to mind. You'll want to have at least five to ten passions listed.

You may be wondering: Why is identifying your passions so important? Because your passions are clues. They are clues to your purpose. Think about it. I said this earlier, but do you really think that God would give you a purpose in life that you hated? I don't think so!

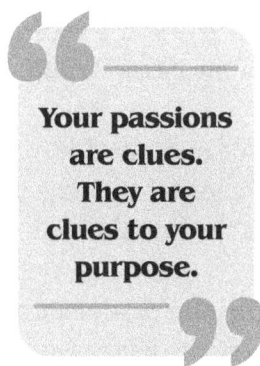

> Your passions are clues. They are clues to your purpose.

Once you have listed all your passions (at least five to ten), focus on the right side of the T, your "Experiences."

We all have many different experiences in life. Some of us have experiences in business, as a parent, in ministry, etc.. So, the same thing applies here. You will want to list out as many of those experiences as possible.

Keep in mind that not all experiences in life are positive. We live in a broken world. Sometimes life is difficult. Others may have caused us pain. We may have lost a loved one, been abused, or have struggled with addiction. Or we may have encountered various setbacks, such as a layoff, bankruptcy, or a divorce.

The thing to remember is that while these experiences may have been painful, and you probably wish you didn't have to experience them, they likely provided you with learning and growing opportunities.

Maybe your faith was strengthened in the process, or you grew closer to a loved one. Or maybe you are still trying to figure out the silver lining.

Either way, you still experienced these events. Regardless of how negative they may have been, they shaped who you are today. So go ahead and write them down too. Again, just like the passion side, you'll want to list at least five to ten experiences to really make this exercise effective. I personally like to fill a page.

MY OWN EXAMPLE

To give you a better idea of how this exercise works, I'll share a few of my passions and experiences with you.

For instance, I love the beach. It's a place where I'm totally at peace. I connect with the ocean in a way I can't even explain. So, the beach is the first thing on my passion list.

I'm also passionate about personal growth and development. I always strive to be the *best* I can be. I thoroughly enjoy reading motivational books, attending seminars, and being around other like-minded people who want to accomplish more for their life.

And I love *pugs*! I have two pugs: Rex and Rosie. They are silly and a never-ending form of entertainment in our house. Not to mention, they bring me and my family so much joy.

I'm also very passionate about my faith, making a difference, and encouraging others to be their best.

Okay, you get the idea.

On the experience side, a few of my experiences include working in sales, being a mom, dancing in my younger years, working for Zig Ziglar, and writing a book.

I've also had some not-so-great experiences, such as moving a few times as a kid and having low self-esteem in my younger years.

I didn't like having those experiences, but that doesn't change the fact that they were a part of my life. So, they also have to go on my list.

Connecting the Dots

Now, back to you. Your two lists show you aspects of who you are, as you are a combination of your passions and your experiences. But when you look closer at what you have written, you'll see that this exercise will help you gain clarity on your story.

Through reflecting on your two lists, you'll find ways you can connect your passions and experiences. You may find you have intersections, whether personally or professionally, that you can share with the world to make a difference in someone else's life.

I'm sure you can see how helpful this exercise would be for authors, as it provides people with a whole list of possible book topics they could write about. But this exercise goes way beyond just finding a book topic. It's designed to help you uncover the real you, the one God created and molded to serve a greater purpose in this world.

Looking at your Passions/Experiences T-Chart, compare your lists and see where you can find a connection or a similarity. Then draw a line from one side of the T to the other side to connect the similarities.

Let's look at my example again. As you remember, one of my passions is personal growth, and one of my experiences is working for Zig Ziglar. Do you see the connection? I'm passionate about personal development and being my best self, plus I've worked for the *master* of personal development and have experience applying his strategies in my own life.

PASSIONS	EXPERIENCES
Beach	Sales
Personal Growth & Development	Mom
Pugs	Dancer
Faith	Worked for Zig Ziglar
Making a Difference	Moved a lot as a child
Encouraging Others	Low self-esteem

A natural way for me to help others would be to share what I learned about personal development from Zig Ziglar while also sharing the experiences, struggles, and obstacles that I faced and ultimately overcame.

In fact, that is what my first book, *Winning In Life Now,* is all about. Because I completed this same exercise, it was very easy for me to write that book. It actually "flew out of me" and onto paper in under three weeks. No kidding!

So, now it's your turn to give it a try. Who knows what kind of breakthroughs you'll find? Where do you see a connection?

If you really put thought and effort into listing all your passions and experiences, you will likely see *many* connections and many things you could share with someone to make a difference. If you look a bit deeper, you may surprise yourself with all that you have to offer this world.

IF NOT YOU, WHO?

You are your story. You can't change your story, but you can identify its meaning. Once you realize what it means, you can share it with others and help them to see the meaning in their life and story too. Who knows, putting it to paper may even give you a new perspective on yourself. When he'd talk about writing books, Zig always used to say, "It's who you become through the process of writing a book that is most important."

> **It's who you become through the process of writing a book that is most important.**
> **–Zig Ziglar**

You see, your story is your journey. Yes, you lived it, but God is the author of your story. You can't change your story, but you can use it to inspire, motivate, and encourage others going through similar journeys.

I know that the idea of sharing your story can be a little scary. It was for me, too, so I totally understand the hesitation. With so many people in this world, I wondered, "*What can I do to make an impact?*" But we are all called to make a difference, and it's not just a suggestion that we let our light shine. It's our responsibility.

I strongly believe that we must tell our stories. If we don't, who will?

Now more than ever before, it's imperative that believers share their stories of God's faithfulness, His love, and His grace. The world desperately needs to hear these stories. I think we all need to share and hear a little more about love, kindness, compassion, and hope instead of the doom and gloom stories that the news and others like to share.

So, I'm asking you … if not *you*, then *who*? And if not *now*, then *when*? God may just be calling you to be an example for others, just like He called Esther "for such a time as this." (Esther 4:14)

WAKE UP, SLEEPING BEAUTY

My good friend Judy Pogue recently wrote an amazing book called *Awaken Sleeping Beauty*. In it, Judy eloquently shares stories of women who have awakened from lives of frustration, busyness, and distraction.

She shares biblical truths that will set us all free from the burdens of daily life and awaken us to the favor, blessings, and love that God has in store for all His precious children. Judy's book is a testament to how God beautifully orchestrates every detail of our lives for us to become all He created us to be.

Judy asked me to write the foreword, which I was honored to do. However, my schedule was so crazy at the time, so I didn't have the luxury to read the whole book in the timeline she requested. I decided to read only the Introduction and Chapter 1 to get a sense of what the book was about, and then write the foreword. But God had a different plan. I couldn't put the book down, and I had a hunch I wasn't reading it as a favor to Judy anymore.

I cleared my schedule for the rest of the day. I read every single word. With every page, it became more apparent that this book wasn't just for women in general—it was for me. *I* needed to wake up.

At that point in my life, my speaking and publishing businesses were going great. I was busy, busy, busy. But I was also asleep, going through the motions. I lost the passion and spirit that got me started, and I settled into complacency and isolation. Judy's book lit a fire in me. It woke me up once again to letting God direct my paths instead of thinking I had to figure it all out. This wasn't the first reminder. And I'm positive it won't be the last.

> **You were created for more. You were created to shine your light, not just some of the time, but all of the time.**

Like me, you were created for more. You were created to shine your light, not just some of the time, but all of the time. I encourage you to decide, once and for all, to "wake up." Right now, you can claim all that God has in store for you.

It's your time. It's time to honor your story and have the courage to share it with the world. And not only the world. You're also sharing the truth with yourself—to heal and validate your thoughts and feelings. Many writers have found putting pen to paper is better than therapy, as they are able to finally process their feelings through their own words. The emotions flow out onto paper and leave room for God to replenish the *seeds of greatness* within! Again, God led you to this book because it is finally *your* time!

CHAPTER SIX

S.H.I.N.E – IDENTIFY WHAT'S HOLDING YOU BACK

"For God gave us a spirit not of fear but of power and love and self-control."
(2 Timothy 1:7 ESV)

I n the Bible, Matthew says, "You are the light of the world." And your light, your story, is not yours alone. It's a gift—a gift from God. He gave it to you so you can give it away like we do with all gifts: to bless others. Essentially, we are just reflecting the light given to us.

I know that some of you might still be struggling with the idea of stepping out in faith to share your story. It could be that something or someone is holding you back. Maybe that something is binding you to a life of mediocrity. Maybe it's self-doubt, worry, procrastination, or fear. Whatever it is, it's time to break those chains and get set free!

How do I know? For starters, I told you about my doubts when it came to sharing my own story through writing a book. And I have many other examples of my thoughts holding me back in my relationships, finances, business, and life. Thankfully, God won't let us stay stuck forever if we're open to change.

Remember, He has plans to prosper us, to give us a future and a hope!

BECOMING UNBOUND

In my profession, I'm blessed and honored to help people become *Book Bound*. I help those willing to step out and share their story, write a book, and ultimately make a difference in the world. But what I see so often is that many of these incredible would-be authors fail to shine their light with their story. Why? Because of the fear, doubt, insecurities, and disbelief that binds them. It's as if they are frozen in fear and can't move forward.

If we are to shine God's light through our story, it's imperative for us to become "unbound" from all that may be holding us back. Only then can we become a blessing to others.

> **If we are to shine God's light through our story, it's imperative for us to become "unbound" from all that may be holding us back.**

Thoughts have power—the power to take you to great levels of success, or the power to keep you stuck in the mud. You may not even realize it, but your mind holds onto early, old input. Some of it was positive, but some of it is no longer valid, even if it was valid at one time.

Many of these thoughts are negative, and most people aren't even aware that they're subconsciously telling themselves things like "I'm not good enough," or "I'm not smart," or "I'll never get out of debt," or "I'll never find someone who truly loves me." Now, just because you're having those thoughts and negative beliefs, doesn't mean they're true.

Zig Ziglar calls those thoughts "garbage dump thinking." While we all have garbage dump thinking from time to time, it doesn't mean we have to keep it. Think to yourself now—what have you been telling yourself all these years, consciously or subconsciously? Or perhaps you have held on to something someone said to you at a very early age that may not have been true. What was it?

Just because someone said it, does not make it true. It's just their opinion. And even if it is true and something that you are not proud of, remember that God's opinion of you is really all that matters, and He is full of grace, love, and forgiveness. We are all flawed in some of our decision-making from time to time, but God feels us worthy of His love and honor no matter what. Why do we feel unworthy and give ourselves less than what God allows for us?

When you hear things from others that are negative about you, make a list of why those thoughts are not true, are no longer true, or are otherwise irrelevant. Now, believe your words! Better yet, believe His words:

> *"But because of his great love for us, God, who is rich in mercy, made us alive with Christ even when we were dead in transgressions—it is by grace you have been saved."*
> (Ephesians 2:4-5)

Accept and forgive your past. Ignore the naysayers. Then, have faith that you can make a new future. Start believing in yourself and what God is creating in you, faults and all.

HOW BELIEFS ARE FORMED

Beliefs can be good or bad. This goes for our spiritual beliefs, the beliefs of how we should treat one another, the beliefs about boundaries, and what's right and what's wrong—all those things we were taught. Believing something doesn't necessarily mean every belief we have is based on fact. Let me explain how this works.

When a child is young, parents, teachers, coaches, ministers, friends, relatives, and any other person of influence in this child's life say things to this child. And then that child accepts it as truth. Why? Because they trust their elders. They accept what these adults or their parents are telling them—especially if it is repeated over years and by the masses. So, the child is also accepting their perception of what's true, even if this person is totally wrong.

Then, unconsciously, this child engrains these beliefs into their subconscious. They build habits according to these beliefs. So, if it's a religious belief, you create habits in your life to accommodate that belief. Whatever your beliefs are, you're putting actions and behaviors in place around those beliefs. You are also vocally spreading it to others within your circle of influence.

> **Whatever your beliefs are, you're putting actions and behaviors in place around those beliefs.**

As children grow into adults, they operate according to dozens of faulty beliefs and habits—but most people aren't consciously aware of this. It isn't until somebody brings it to their attention that they realize it is a wrong belief. You don't know anything different. It's what you've always known, and you're operating or behaving around these false beliefs.

For example, if someone tells you you're not smart, and you believe them, then you might not try in school. Maybe you never graduated high school and didn't bother going to college because you believed that only smart people would do things like that. Your behaviors are wrapped around that belief, and that's why you didn't push forward.

So, as an adult, we operate under all these false, limiting beliefs, and then we set invisible boundaries for our lives. It's all in our subconscious. It's not like we're sitting around thinking: "I really want to hold myself back." That's not what's going on.

I like to compare our negative beliefs to a sliding glass door. Have you ever seen someone walk directly into a glass door or window? Or have you done so yourself? It's usually accompanied by a big *thump* and can embarrass even the best of us. If it's happened to you, you know exactly what I mean. It's like all of a sudden that glass door just *appeared* out of nowhere. But the reality is that it was there all along. No matter how much you deny its presence, it doesn't change the fact that the glass door will stop you in your tracks every time if you don't open it. It's the same with our beliefs. We may not know we have negative beliefs, but that won't stop them from holding us back.

THE EARTH IS WHAT?

Let's use the earth is flat as an example. Stick with me on this, because it may seem a little far-fetched.

Let's just say, for example, that when you were a baby, you were raised by a wonderful family, and this family believed that the earth was flat. Your aunts, uncles, cousins, grandparents, neighbors, friends at school … they all believed the earth was flat, too. So, your entire life that was your truth: the earth is flat. There was no other way about it.

Then, as an adult, you're in a conversation with a co-worker and the topic of the earth comes up. You say, "The earth is flat."

This person looks at you oddly and says, "Are you crazy? The earth isn't flat. The earth is round."

But you're adamant that it is indeed flat, and you're willing to take on that argument because you know you're right. After all, that's what you were always told. It was drilled into your head, day in, day out, all throughout your life, so it must be true. But is it?

We obviously know the earth is not flat. It's round. So, this belief that you're willing to bet your life on is based on falsehoods. It's a lie. It's *not* true.

Okay, what's the point in all of this? The point is, the same applies to what you are telling yourself. Whatever you believe, whatever you may have heard your whole life about yourself or your situation, doesn't make it true.

Perhaps through the years somebody has said something hurtful to you that you held on to as truth. Things like, "You can't do anything right," or, "You're not smart." "You'll never make it in the world." "You'll never be as good as your brother or your sister." And so on.

I used "the earth is flat" as an example, and yes, it's a little bit exaggerated. But the example is the same for those of us who have held on to false beliefs most of our lives.

A couple of years ago, at one of our *Book Bound* workshops, an attendee shared a story with the group that impacted me and everyone else in a deep way. We had just gone through a belief activity, and a gentleman in the group stood up to share some of his own negative beliefs, one of which was seeing himself as the "fat boy." We were all perplexed because he was a thin, healthy man. No one would have ever thought of him as overweight.

But because it was a belief that he had held on to for most of his life, it impacted how he saw himself, even years after losing the weight of his youth. After going through this exercise and realizing that what he "believed" was not based on fact, he proudly declared to the group that for the first time in sixty-plus years, he was no longer that "fat boy." There wasn't a dry eye in the room! You see, nothing changes until our own beliefs about ourselves change too.

> **Nothing changes until our own beliefs about ourselves change too.**

Bottom line—to SHINE your light, you first must recognize what's holding you back. Then, you must embrace its impact on your past and decide for a more transparent future based upon fact, not fiction. Then, and only then, can you be all that you were created to be.

WHO DO YOU THINK YOU ARE?

I want to do a little exercise to help you identify all those negative, limiting beliefs, the ones that are not serving you. The ones that may be spinning around in your mind but may not be based on truth.

Grab a sheet of paper (or use the space provided below) to list as many thoughts and negative beliefs as possible that you have told yourself or held on to most of your life.

These could be thoughts about business, relationships, money, success, etc. Some examples could be "I'm lazy" or "I'll never have enough money" or "I'm not good enough," etc. These thoughts are not serving you or God's purpose for your life any longer. If you don't identify what they are, then you can't overcome them.

MY BELIEFS

Take the time now to write down all the negative thoughts and beliefs that have been going through your mind throughout your life—thoughts about yourself, your relationships, finances, etc.

....

....

....

....

....

....

....

....

I'll share another personal story of my own. For most of my life, I had a negative limiting belief that I wasn't good enough. I don't know where that came from. I had a wonderful childhood and a supportive family, but for whatever reason, I didn't think I measured up. Who was I even measuring myself up against? I'm not even sure.

That negative limiting belief kept me from being the person I was created to be for many years. It literally held me captive without me even knowing it. But then one day I decided to do this same exercise to eliminate my false belief. I decided once and for all to grab hold of the real truth: the truth that I was beautifully and wonderfully made, loved by God, and made for a purpose.

Therefore, any limits on my life—the ones that truly exist (like the fact that I am not a great cook) —were purposefully allowed there by God during this season. And I know that He can completely change my limits in a split second, so I don't dwell on them. Instead, I look at them like I would any key to my rightful path. The limits may be required for me to have a particular experience I need to grow. And so, the limits may be part of my own perfection! See, if I was a great cook, I may never have written a book. My purpose does not involve cooking, so that gift may have just been a distraction.

Sometimes, there are beliefs that have a seed of truth in them, and we expand upon and allow them to be a disability for us. We feed the seed until it takes on a life of its own … one of destruction. For instance, we have all heard about there being a glass ceiling for women. Yes, there are instances of this, but there are also instances of this not being someone's reality. Fear of this being our reality could be just as debilitating—whether it is the truth or not—because we can let that fear hold us back. So, even in cases where there is no true glass ceiling, we create a fictitious one with our own fear feeding itself.

If this is your experience, fight your fears by rejecting them. Lean on the Word and on God to show you the way. We forget that God is in control and will give us all we need for His purposes for our lives. If this is true for you or you feel it just the same, tell yourself that you will be that woman who shatters that ceiling with His might behind you!

You are beautifully and wonderfully made. To really shine and be all that you were created to be, you first have to let go of what's holding you back. Let go, and let God manage the mess. After all, as I've said before, in your mess is your message!

TIME TO TAKE OUT THE TRASH

> **You are beautifully and wonderfully made. To really shine and be all that you were created to be, you first have to let go of what's holding you back.**

Let me ask you a question. If I were to come over to your house and throw a huge bag of garbage—filled with dirty diapers, rotten fruit, and all kinds of disgusting things—on your living room floor, would you be mad? Would you kick me out of your house and tell me to never come back? Of course you would! You would never let anyone treat you so badly!

So then why do we allow other people to throw that same kind of trash into our minds and let them get away with it? Just because they said it, doesn't make it true. It's garbage! Even if there is a seed of truth, it's still garbage because it's no longer serving you.

It's time to take all those negative thoughts—thoughts you have allowed to take up residency in your mind for way too long—and kick them to the curb! They don't serve you anymore, so literally and figuratively take that list of negative beliefs and throw it where that stuff belongs, in the trash!

SPEAK THE TRUTH

Now that you released your negative thoughts, it's time to replace them with the truth. You do this through positive self-talk and biblical affirmations.

The purpose of positive self-talk is to turn those negative thoughts around and sell yourself on *you*! Instead of all the negative things you were saying about yourself, now you're going to say positive things. This will allow your mind to focus on what is true. And when you fill your mind with what you want in life, it has no choice but to follow.

> **When you fill your mind with what you want in life, it has no choice but to follow.**

For affirmations to be strong, they must be positive and stated in the present tense (I am, I can). For example, "I'm always late" can be replaced with "I arrive five minutes early wherever I go." Or "I'm not good enough" can be replaced with "I'm perfect just the way I am." If you find it a stretch to say and believe that you are perfect, start with baby steps by declaring what He has told you … "*I am perfect in the eyes of God,*" as shared In Ezekiel 28:12 (NIV).

POSITIVE AFFIRMATIONS

Write down several positive affirmations to replace the negative self-talk you identified in our last exercise:

....

....

....

....

....

....

....

Once you have your list of positive affirmations, read them aloud twice each day—once in the morning and once in the evening—for the next thirty days. Better yet, place sticky notes all around you with the positive affirmations, and repeat them each time you see them. Put the affirmations on your computer screen and phone screen saver! Create posters, refrigerator magnets, or key chains with your affirmations on them. The more positive words that go into your mind and ears, the better!

If negative thoughts have consumed your thinking for a long time, then you may not believe everything you're saying at first. But don't give up! Eventually, you will replace those negative beliefs with *the truth* and see transformation happen in ways you cannot even imagine. As Zig would say, "We're just telling the truth in advance."

I did this many years ago, long before I had the courage to step out in faith and write my book. One of my good friends was going through the process to become a certified coach, and as part of her certification she needed to coach a couple of people for free. I was happy to help her, but what I received was so much more than what I could have possibly done to help her.

> **Eventually, you will replace those negative beliefs with the truth and see transformation happen in ways you cannot even imagine.**

The first session she took me through focused on our beliefs and how they affect all areas of our lives. She had me identify my limiting thoughts and then create affirmation cards that stated the opposite of my negative belief. At first, I didn't buy into the positive version, but she told me to look myself in the mirror and read those affirmations out loud once in the morning and again at night. I did this for thirty days, and I was amazed to see the transformation that took place.

Of course, I still struggled with negative thoughts, but reading the positive affirmations eventually took root. I was able to make adjustments to my attitude and how I approached life. I love those affirmation cards. In fact, all these years later, I still have those cards tucked in my Bible. I pull them out from time to time to remind myself of who I am, Whose I am, and that I was created for so much more.

Running After the Truth

Another great example of the power of our minds is the story of Roger Bannister. Roger was the very first person to ever run a mile in under four minutes.

Before him, it was basically believed across the entire world that the human body was physically incapable of doing such a thing.

Well, Roger Bannister was a medical student, and he held a totally different belief. He was fueled by his faith. He believed he could overcome his obstacles. He believed his body was capable of running a mile quicker than four minutes, and he wasn't afraid to take action.

He had this belief, he had a dream, and it became his reality. Roger Bannister not only broke the four-minute mile, but he triggered a new belief in people all around the world.

Before that time, and because no one thought it was possible to run a mile so quickly, nobody bothered trying. But within forty-six days of Roger Bannister breaking this amazing four-minute mile barrier, somebody else beat the record.

And then, within two years, more than fifty people ran a sub four-minute mile. Today, thousands of people have done it.

So, what happened in 1954, when Roger Bannister first hit that major milestone, that hadn't happened before? What allowed him to achieve this?

Obviously, it wasn't the physical human body that changed. It was the human belief that changed. He went into that situation believing he could achieve it, and he did. And, in doing so, he inspired others to do the same.

I experienced that same thing when I shifted my belief and wrote my first book. I never imagined that this decision would have a ripple effect on so many other people, including my parents and my brother. Each of them became authors shortly after I started down this path, and countless others have told me how I inspired them to share their story. I'm sure there are many more that I don't even know about, which is incredibly humbling. I'm so grateful that God used me to encourage His other children, as I have prayed to Him to do.

Are you one of them? If you were inspired in some way to write a book as a result of meeting me, hearing me speak, or reading one of my books, then I'd love to hear from you. It's not to bolster my own confidence, but rather to give glory to God for giving us the power to make a difference when we share our stories. You can email me at Support@SHINEThroughYourStory.com or share your SHINE Story at www.SHINEThroughYourStory.com.

> **Start speaking what you want out of life, and let those words guide your future.**

Words have power. What we tell ourselves matters. Start speaking what you want out of life, and let those words guide your future. If you are not in a place where you know what to request for yourself just yet, don't let that deter you. Remember, God knows your heart and He will reveal it to you in the right season.

TAKE UP YOUR SWORD

The positive self-talk affirmations that you wrote down are critical to changing your beliefs, but you must also affirm who you are—who God says you are—by speaking the truth about your identity. We do this through Biblical affirmations.

A couple of years ago, I went through Priscilla Shirer's Bible study, *Armor of God,* and it changed my life. It's based on Ephesians 6:10-19.

"Finally, be strong in the Lord and in the strength of His might. Put on the full armor of God, so that you will be able to stand firm against the schemes of the devil. For our struggle is not against flesh and blood, but against the rulers, against the powers, against the world forces of this darkness, against the spiritual forces of wickedness in the heavenly places. Therefore, take up the full armor of God, so that you will be able to resist in the evil day, and having done everything, to stand firm. Stand firm therefore, having girded your loins with truth and having put on the breastplate of righteousness. And having shod your feet with the preparation of the gospel of peace; in addition to all, taking up the shield of faith with which you will be able to extinguish all the flaming arrows of the evil one. And take the helmet of salvation and the sword of the Spirit, which is the word of God. With all prayer and petition, pray at all times in the Spirit, and with this in view, be on the alert with all perseverance and petition for all the saints, and pray..."
(Ephesians 6:10-19 NRSV)

If you've never done one of Priscilla's studies or read any of her books, I highly recommend that you do. She can speak truth so clearly and make complex biblical concepts simple for people all around the world.

Priscilla and I also worked together at Ziglar, Inc., back in the '90s, and I can tell you that everything she says or does has one purpose … and that purpose is to glorify God.

Priscilla talks about the spiritual battle that is at work around us every day of our lives. We may not see this battle happening physically, but rest assured, there are powers of darkness doing everything they can to take us down.

But there is also good news! The Bible says we've already won the war and have the final victory in the name of Jesus! Plus, God has given us strategic weapons with which to fight back: weapons like the belt of truth, the breastplate of righteousness, the shoes of peace, the shield of faith, the helmet of salvation, and the sword of the spirit.

This armor and these weapons are critical for us to "put on" so that we can stand firm against attacks. The first six weapons we have available to us are "defensive" strategies. Meaning once the enemy takes a hit at us, we have these tools to fight back.

But there is one piece of armor that Paul actually describes in Ephesians 6, and it's the only "offensive" weapon that we have in our arsenal. Paul is telling us not to just take a defensive posture in this war. We must also prepare ourselves in advance using the sword of the Spirit, which is the Word of God. When we speak the truth about who we are in Christ, we have the power to overcome whatever forces come against us.

If you are struggling with fear or you need some additional encouragement, I suggest you read over some of the biblical affirmations that Priscilla shares in this study. She's titled these affirmations "My Inheritance and Identity in Christ."

"My Inheritance and Identity in Christ"
(Excerpt from *Armor of God*, by Priscilla Shirer)

"I am a child of God" – John 1:12
"I have peace with God" – Romans 5:1
"I have access to God's wisdom" – James 1:5
"I am helped by God" – Hebrews 4:16
"I am not condemned by God" – Romans 8:1
"I am Christ's ambassador" – 2 Corinthians 5:20
"I am completely forgiven" – Colossians 1:14
"I am tenderly loved by God" – Jeremiah 31:3
"I am the light of the world" – Matthew 5:14
"I am Christ's friend" – John 15:5
"I am chosen by Christ to bear fruit" – John 15:6
"I am a joint heir with Christ, sharing his
inheritance with him" – Romans 8:17
"I am a member of Christ's body" – 1 Corinthians 12:27
"I am chosen by God, holy and dearly loved" – Colossians 3:12
"I am a child of the light" – 1 Thessalonians 5:5
"I am holy, and I share in God's heavenly calling" – Hebrews 3:1
"I am a member of a chosen race, a royal priesthood, a holy nation, a people
for God's own passion and created to sing his praises" – 1 Peter 2:9-10
"I am firmly rooted and built up in Christ" – Colossians 2:7
"I have the mind of Christ" – 1 Corinthians 2:16
"I may approach God with boldness, freedom, and confidence" – Ephesians 3:12
"I have been given a spirit of power, love, and self-discipline" – 2 Timothy 1:7
"I am a prince or princess in God's kingdom" – John 1:12; 1 Timothy 6:15
"I have direct access to God through the Holy Spirit" – Ephesians 2:18
"I am assured that all things are working together for good" – Romans 8:28
"I cannot be separated from the love of God" – Romans 8:35
"I am confident that the good work that God has begun in me will be perfected"
– Philippians 1:6
"I am God's workmanship" – Ephesians 2:10
"I can do all things through Christ, who gives me the strength I need"
– Philippians 4:13

As believers and followers of Jesus, these scriptures hold true for you and me as well. Declare these biblical affirmations daily, along with the ones you created in this chapter. Do so with confidence, and trust that God will always be there to help you with your battles.

OVERCOMING PROCRASTINATION

Our beliefs may be the main culprit holding us back and keeping us stuck, but there is another nemesis that will stop you in your tracks if you don't get it under control. It's the dreaded "P" word: Procrastination.

I know about procrastination all to well. In fact, I procrastinated when it came to getting this book over the finish line. Thankfully, God didn't allow me to stay in my comfort zone, and I hope He doesn't let you stay stuck either.

There are a lot of reasons why people procrastinate. I know that all of us do it at one time or another, and boy, are we ever good at justifying it the more we do it! But what I want you to start thinking about is *where* you are procrastinating and *why*.

If you want to get a handle on this thing called procrastination, you must take action. To help you with this, I'm going to give you four tips that I know you can implement right away to rid yourself of procrastination and instead BECOME A FINISHER!

> **Fear is the opposite of faith. You can't have both at the same time.**

TIP #1: Identify What's Holding You Back

In most cases, what we procrastinate on boils down to something we fear. Whether it's fear of failure or fear of success, in our subconscious it's the same blockade holding us back. It's imperative for you to get real, identify that fear, call it out, and let it go once and for all. Remember, fear is the opposite of faith. You can't have both at the same time. It's a choice, and the choice is yours to make now.

Ultimately, what's really holding us back is ourselves. We know what to do and maybe even how to do it, but we just cannot take that step. We create a plethora of excuses to tell ourselves and keep us from living big lives: "I am too old," "I am too busy," or "That is too hard!" I know it can be scary, but when you really think about it, not growing in life should be even scarier to you. Pull yourself out of your *Groundhog Day* for something more!

Think of life like one big game of Escape Room. When we are stuck somewhere, there are always clues to open the doors that will move our lives forward—if we just look for them in the right places. God is nudging and guiding us along if we will just take His lead. The key to escaping the past or opening a door of discovery for our new future can be *your* story! This book can be your key to a door taking you to the next level in the game of life. Ready to open that door?

TIP #2: Practice Discipline and Motivation

Nothing changes if nothing changes, and anything worth pursuing will take hard work. I know that's not a popular answer, but it is the truth when it comes to achieving anything great in life.

> **Nothing changes if nothing changes, and anything worth pursuing will take hard work.**

Same goes for making a difference. You must be intentional, disciplined, and proactive in finding opportunities to share your story.

But there is good news!

When you are doing something that is within your passion and purpose, something that you love to do, and you're making a difference for others, then your passion will pull you. You don't have to push it.

You may be working hard, but if it's tied to your passion and purpose in life, it will never *feel* like work.

TIP #3: Dust Off Your Dreams

What was your dream when you were younger? It could have been ten years ago, or even forty years ago. Think back to a time in your life before you had responsibilities—before you faced rejection. What lit you up? What got you excited? Was it cooking? Was it teaching? Was it writing or singing? Was it personal development, like me? If it was truly tied to your passion, then most likely it will still light you up today.

When I was eighteen and met Zig Ziglar at his *Born To Win* conference, I wanted to be like him. I had the dream of one day speaking at conferences and sharing my own message of hope and encouragement. And now, I'm so beyond honored and blessed to be able to write and speak to people all over the world. Here I am fulfilling my purpose all these years later. That's the power of a dream.

If you really want to step into your greatness and be the best that you can be in your business, in your family or personal life, then go back and dust off your dreams.

TIP #4: Start Living Now

> *"Don't put it off, do it now!*
> *Don't rest until you do."*
> (Proverbs 6:4 NLT)

I know it sounds cliché, but life is short. Think about it … how fast last summer flew by, how the holidays were over just about the time they started, and how your childhood is a fleeting memory. Yet, many people live like they'll live forever, pushing their most important dreams to the back burner.

We think we'll get to it someday—when we're not so busy or when we have more money. Or when the kids are in school, when the kids are out of school, or when the kids are married ... Or when the grandkids are grown, when we retire ... you get the idea. The truth is, we will always be busy; we will always find something to fill up our time.

Life Is Short

In 1999, our family suffered a devastating loss. My mother-in-law, Cindy Abernathy, died in a car accident. I can't begin to describe the pain and devastation we all went through.

I was nine months pregnant with our first son—Cindy's first grandchild. He was the joy of everyone's lives, and we all couldn't wait until he arrived. The night before the accident, I went to see my doctor, and to my delight he said I was already well on my way. He thought I would probably deliver that coming weekend. I can remember calling my in-laws to tell them the wonderful news. The baby was finally coming! He would be here in just a few days!

Cindy was scheduled to go on a business trip that weekend, but she was more than willing to cancel it to be with us. It was a relatively new job for my mother-in-law, and I knew it was important to her, so I told her I'd call her in the morning to let her know how I felt. If contractions started increasing, Cindy said she'd cancel the trip.

I was never able to make that call. The date was Thursday, September 9, 1999. I had great expectations about that date because I thought it would be cool if my son was born on 9-9-99. However, that date was set for a very different event.

My parents were the ones to give me the news. My father-in-law was concerned how it would affect me and the baby, so he thought it best if I heard the news in person rather than over the phone. At the time, my in-laws lived a few hours from us, so my father-in-law was not able to tell me right away. He called my parents, and they immediately drove to my house.

There is no way to describe how I felt when I heard the news. Chris and his mom were very close. I couldn't fathom the thought of having to tell him that his mother was gone, and that she'd never get to meet his first-born son. Yet this was to be my responsibility, as I had been told first about the tragedy.

The rest of that day was a blur. Family members gathered to grieve and discuss plans. In tears, I immediately called my doctor and asked for help.

I was so excited about having this baby, but now all I wanted to do was stop him from coming. I couldn't bear the thought of Chris having to welcome his newborn baby and bury his mother on the same day.

Because I was so overcome by grief, and these feelings could easily trigger labor, it was important to keep myself as calm as possible. I did not want my baby to feel the stress of the loss, but so much was out of my control at that moment. The doctor advised that I stay quietly lying down at all times. This wasn't easy, but I wanted to do whatever I could for both my husband and our son.

My prayers were answered. Austin was born thirteen days after Chris' mother died. To me, it was a miracle: A baby that was expected to arrive in just a day or two somehow held back for thirteen more days. I have no doubt this miracle came because of a wonderful doctor and a lot of prayer. Thirteen days is not much time, but it was enough to separate these two dramatically different life-altering events.

> I learned how quickly life can change, and how short our time on earth really is. No one is guaranteed even one more day before our time is up.

The preciousness of life becomes so apparent during those moments of departure and arrival. Priorities suddenly become crystal clear. I learned how quickly life can change, and how short our time on earth really is. No one is guaranteed even *one more day* before our time is up.

To truly shine our lights and share our stories, we need to get off "Someday Isle." Someday I'll do this; someday I'll do that. We need to take action on the things that matter. We need to start living now, while we're still in the living years.

One Story at a Time

I love the Bible verse in 2 Timothy where the Apostle Paul is encouraging Timothy, his young protégé. Paul writes:

> *"For the Spirit God gave us does not make us timid,*
> *but gives us power, love, and self-discipline."*
> (2 Timothy 1:7)

You have the power to choose your thoughts and overcome your fears. Stop worrying, doubting, or being afraid of sharing your story with the world. God will always be with you, and He will give you the strength you need.

Early on in my journey, I felt fear and doubt about sharing my story, but God gave me the grace and strength to share it anyway. I listened to Him and obeyed what I knew God was calling me to do.

I could never have imagined that one act of obedience would have opened me up to the many opportunities I now have, including to serve Him by helping others share their own stories.

I'm so passionate about inspiring, equipping, and sending forth other believers to share their stories. It's what's needed most in the world today.

We all have stories of God's love, favor, protection, provision, and faithfulness. I believe that together we can change the world one story at a time.

You are called to walk with God. You are called to shine your light. And God will always equip those He calls. It may not be easy, but if He's calling you *to it*, He will bring you *through it*.

Jesus called the disciples to tell their stories. Is He calling you to do the same? If so, you should obey His commands. Even if you feel the fear, it's okay. He will be there for you. It's time to step out in faith, identify, and overcome what's holding you back. Follow the call and say, like Isaiah, *"Here am I. Send me!"* (Isaiah 6:8)

> **I believe that together we can change the world one story at a time.**

CHAPTER SEVEN

S.H.I.N.E – NOW IS THE TIME TO WRITE YOUR STORY

*"This is what the Lord, the God of Israel, says: Write in a book
all the words I've spoken to you."*
(Jeremiah 30:2)

I love journals. I've been writing in journals since I was a little girl. As I grew older, I started packing up all my old journals in a box, never to be read again.

But for some reason, I recently felt this urge to go back and reread what I wrote all those years ago. And I'm so glad I did!

At first, these old journal entries were mostly about my day, the boys I liked, and what I had for dinner. Nothing too deep or meaningful. Still, it was so much fun to go back and read what I thought when I was in elementary school, junior high, and high school.

I cringe now at some of my writings because, let's be honest, the mind of a pre-teen isn't exactly refined. But I've also found many reasons to smile at the honesty, vulnerability, and naiveté in my early writings. It makes me wonder what I will think as I read this book 20 years from now.

It also was very eye-opening to me because, as I reread these journals, I realized I'm exactly the same person I was then … just a much better version of myself, thankfully.

> **Our soul is our soul, and we're created in the image of God, even if we don't see it.**

It's amazing to me that the core of who we are doesn't change that much, even if we think we've improved or matured. Our soul is our soul, and we're created in the image of God, even if we don't see it. I didn't see it when I was young, and I have moments when I struggle to see it now, but it's there. I'm in Him and He's in me, and that doesn't change. And the only reason I know this is because I wrote it down and can go back to be reminded of it—just like the disciples. If they hadn't realized that now is to the time to write, where would we be?

QUIET TIME

My grown up journal entries began when I was a freshman in college. I was living in West Hall at the University of North Texas with my two roommates, Kimberly and Tara. Kimberly was a very strong Christian. The way she spoke and acted was all very new to me. I was a believer and had been since I was in the second grade (more on that story later), but Kimberly had a real, deep, and personal relationship with Jesus that was unlike anything I had ever experienced.

Our first week living together in the dorm, I noticed that Kimberly would stay up a little later than Tara and I did. She was in the top bunk and would keep her light on. I wondered what she was doing up there, so I asked her the next day.

Kimberly told me that she was doing her "Quiet Time." She said that every night, before bed, she would read a Bible verse and then journal about what she learned, felt, or experienced with it.

I had done similar things during high school but was never consistent with it. But then Kimberly taught me how to do it this way. Every night, no matter how tired I was, I would do my *Quiet Time* too.

I had a devotional someone gave me called *God Calling*. So, every night I'd read the verse and paragraph for that specific date and then start my journal entry. Every single entry, from that day on, started with, "Thank you, Jesus ..."

Looking back, I'm in awe of the things I felt and shared with God each of those nights. Although each entry began with gratitude, I also wrote about my pain and struggles. To be honest, I had forgotten about so much of that until I reread these entries.

Back then, I was struggling with my identity and self-esteem, and I was really yearning for more. But I didn't know what "more" was or what I was missing in my life.

I thought that what I really needed was a boyfriend. I didn't have a solid boyfriend throughout high school—just a few dates here and there, but nothing really meaningful. I longed for that kind of relationship.

But now that I'm older, and as I look back at my journal entries, I recognize that what I was really longing for was a more meaningful relationship with Jesus.

MONDAY MORNING DEVOTIONS

A couple of years ago, I was asked to lead *Devotions* at the Ziglar offices. This is a very special meeting that has been going on for decades, so I was excited to stay engaged with everyone there. I first experienced these *Devotions* meetings when I was a twenty-two-year-old starting out at Ziglar Inc.

Every Monday morning at 7:30 a.m., we'd have our *"most important meeting of the week,"* as Zig would say. It was an optional meeting, but pretty much everyone in the office attended.

This was all new to me. I wasn't used to talking about God at work, or really anywhere outside of church. Still, I was intrigued by the thought, and I attended the meetings anyway.

I think part of me attended those devotional meetings initially because I was a people pleaser, and I didn't want to be seen as "that girl" for not attending. I didn't want to be looked down upon or be thought of negatively. After all, I love God and always have. Again, it was the whole "relationship" part that I didn't quite understand yet. During the devotion, I noticed hands going up, whispers to Jesus as we prayed, and folks kneeling at their chairs in reverence to God.

It was beautiful, but at the same time, it made me a little uncomfortable because we didn't do it that way at my church. I came from a very faithful, strong Catholic family. Growing up, we had worshiped God in more private ways.

Now, I'm not saying one worship style is better than the other. It's just that initially I was not very comfortable with the more "out there" style of worship that I had seen at Ziglar. Week by week, I came to love it.

So, back to my story about being asked to do *Devotions* in 2017. This was a good twenty years after working at Ziglar, and I was honored to have been asked to speak again.

I had prepared my teaching points for the day, but something was stirring inside, making me doubt that what I had prepared was what I was actually supposed to share.

I knew that what I was originally planning to present was good (at least I thought it was), but still something was gnawing at me to change it.

That's when I clearly heard God say to me, *"Tell them how we met."* What? Tell them how we met? Huh? What do you mean?

Inwardly, I asked God for more specifics, but I didn't get any more detail, just to "tell them how we met." I sat there puzzled. Do I even remember?

As I was sitting at my kitchen table, looking out the window, I instantly recalled everything in vivid detail. So, I grabbed my pen and started to write about my first encounter with God.

OPENING THE DOOR

I don't think I had thought about our first "meeting" since I was a little girl. I know I definitely never told anyone about it. It was just between me and Jesus … and I thought it was going to stay that way—at least until the day He told me otherwise.

> She saw something in me that I couldn't quite see in myself at the time—or for many more years to come, for that matter. She saw my light … a light that I didn't even know existed, and yet it was still there, flickering.

I was in the second grade at Saint Joseph's Catholic School. I have some good memories of private school, and some not so good ones. But second grade brings back very happy memories for me.

I had Sister Angela as one of my teachers, and I absolutely loved her. Best of all, she loved me too. In fact, I don't think I have ever had a teacher since then that made me feel as seen, heard, and most importantly, loved, like Sister Angela did.

She saw something in me that I couldn't quite see in myself at the time—or for many more years to come, for that matter. She saw my light … a light that I didn't even know existed, and yet it was still there, flickering.

She favored me, and her attention opened up my heart to hear what it was she had to say. She talked about Jesus—a lot.

One day, she was teaching on Revelation 3:20 ESV. This Bible verse says,

> *"Behold, I stand at the door and knock. If anyone hears my voice and opens the door, I will come in to him and eat with him, and he with me."*

She continued by saying that Jesus is always there for us, and He's waiting for us to open the door to Him.

She showed us a picture of Jesus standing at the door, but with no handle on His side—only on our side. The only way for Him to enter our lives is if *we* open the door and invite Him in. It totally made sense. And then she said, "Jesus is here right now. Will you let Him in?" That's when it hit me.

I remember thinking, *"Wait, Jesus is here? Right now? What?"* I was looking all around the classroom, as if He was just going to appear out of nowhere. I was so excited! Even though I didn't see Him physically, in that moment I *knew* that He was there!

I was sitting in one of those old parochial school desks—the kind that is metal and wood, all one piece, with an opening under the seat for books. That desk had only a *tiny little* seat, just big enough for my seven-year-old frame. But in that moment, knowing that Jesus was "in the house," I literally scooted over in my seat, as far as I could, up against the metal bar. I patted the bottom of my chair and invited Him in.

> In my spirit I said, 'Jesus, you can come sit with me.' And, you know what? He did!

In my spirit I said, *"Jesus, you can come sit with me."* And, you know what? He did! It's hard for me to really explain how

I knew, but at a deep gut level, I had no doubt He was right there sitting with me at my desk.

And funny enough, I don't remember being amazed, surprised, or even shocked that the King of Kings, the Lord of Lords, the Son of God, was sitting with *me*. It seemed so normal. It felt so right. I remember feeling so happy, joyful, and loved. I had found my very best friend.

From that moment on, I have always known that Jesus was with me, and I knew that He'd show up if I needed Him. It was like I had this "secret weapon," this "bodyguard" that would be there in a moment's notice to show up on my behalf. Of course, I didn't fully understand the depth of it all, but I did know He'd be there for me when I needed Him. And He's there for you too.

Looking back, I can clearly see the hand of God in my life, especially during my teen and early adolescent years. There were plenty of times I'd put myself in precarious situations or with people I shouldn't have been with, and in those moments, when I knew I needed protection or support, I'd say, *"Jesus, I love you and I need you now."* And He'd come to my rescue. Never in physical or audible form, but in my spirit, I knew that He was there to protect me.

It was a crazy confidence I had in Christ. I would call on Him, and He would show up. But I kept it a secret—even from my closest friends.

MY WALKS WITH GOD

Most of my friends knew I was spiritual. I went to church faithfully every Wednesday and Sunday; I led a Sunday school class at church while I was in high school; I attended church retreats, and I was very active in my faith. Most people knew that part of me, but they didn't know the inward part. They didn't know that I *knew* Jesus. And since I didn't want people to think I was *crazy*, I kept it to myself.

My very best friend in high school lived on my street, and there were many times I'd walk down to her house at night alone. It was a safe neighborhood, so being alone was never an issue, and I was never ever *truly* alone. I'd have the most amazing experiences on those walks. That's when I'd talk to God.

> **I'd look up at the stars, and I'd feel this unexplainable joy, peace, and reassurance that He was watching over me and that He loved me.**

I don't remember exactly what I'd say, but night after night, as I took that three-minute walk, I would listen as God spoke to me in my spirit. He'd comfort me and let me know that He was there for me. I'd look up at the stars, and I'd feel this unexplainable joy, peace, and reassurance that He was watching over me and that He loved me.

> *"And the peace of God, which transcends all understanding, will guard your hearts and your minds in Christ Jesus."*
> (Philippians 4:7)

I loved those nights with God. I still do.

You may be asking, *"What's the point of this story? What does your first encounter with God at the age of seven have anything to do with me and my story?"*

Well … I'm not sure. I felt I was supposed to share it because that's how God works … in and through our stories. We were created to connect, and we connect with others when we share ourselves—our true selves—through our stories.

Connecting with one another, and the transparency and vulnerability that it requires, can be a scary thing. It has always been like that for me. But thankfully, God opened my eyes to see that our story, even the hard parts, is all part of our larger purpose, which is to ultimately glorify God with the wonderful things He's done for us.

Our story is our own recounting of God's faithfulness. *Our* story is really *His* story, a beautiful love story of Jesus' willingness to die on the cross for us so that we can live ... and live abundantly.

That's why believers need to document their stories.

Just think about it. We wouldn't have our faith today if it weren't for believers like Moses, David, Matthew, Paul, and Peter documenting their stories. Because they documented their stories, their lives have encouraged generations of believers over the last several thousand years!

His Faithfulness Is True

Now, back to my story about college and when I started to journal. That's when my walks with God in high school turned into full-blown conversations, all thanks to my writing. I wrote about my day, my dreams, my fears, my desires, and He loved hearing every single detail about my life.

He was there when I was sad and when I was happy. He listened to me, and each night as I wrote to Him, He *always* showed up. God is so good, and He is so patient. He will never leave you or forsake you. He will pursue you because you are exactly what He desires.

> God is so good, and He is so patient. He will never leave you or forsake you. He will pursue you because you are exactly what He desires.

That's what He did for me. My journal entries are filled with stories of God's love and His companionship. Over and over and over again, His faithfulness and His goodness proved true in my life. But I couldn't always see it in the moment, and I didn't always appreciate all the greatness around me.

It's in looking back and rereading my journals that I see God's faithfulness and His never-ending love for me. The real me! And yet even with all this "proof" of His love, I still had doubts and didn't feel like I deserved it. I'd subconsciously ask, *"Why would God want to pursue me? Why would He care about little old me? Who am I that I'd get the attention of the Almighty God?"* Those may sound like some of your questions too.

Jesus wants us to know that He loves us, no matter what, and that He will always be there for us. He doesn't want us to worry or be fearful about anything. Instead, He only wants us to trust in Him.

Looking back, I can clearly see that God has been with me all of my life. He stayed by my side even when I ignored Him and denied Him. He was there when I was sad or when I felt bad about myself. He was with me as I struggled with my identity and where I fit in. He was with me when I was afraid or in danger. He was there when I experienced loss of a loved one. He was also there in the good times, like the birth of my children—the birth of His miracles in my life! He is also here with me now, as I write this. He is also with you—right where you are, right now!

> **The bottom line is this: God never leaves our sides, and He never will.**

The bottom line is this: God never leaves our side, and He never will.

"Write in a Book …"

A couple of years ago, the idea of connecting with God through writing became crystal clear for me.

As I mentioned, I've always journaled, and that's how I best hear from God. I also help people to write books, but I never really put it all together and recognized the significance of *why* we should write until January 2019.

I was hosting my *Book Bound By The Sea* seminar in Destin, Florida, when the revelation hit me. It was the morning of the third and final day of the event. We offered an optional Sunday morning devotional for those who wanted to come together as a group an hour before the actual seminar sessions started.

I've been doing these devotionals at *Book Bound* on and off for years, so this was not an unusual occurrence. But it ended up being a morning I'll never forget, and it's what ended up being the catalyst for writing this book.

We had over seventy attendees at this seminar, and as you can imagine, there was plenty to do to prepare for and lead a successful three-day event. Every detail was planned out weeks in advance, but an hour before I was to lead everyone in this devotional on the third day, I realized I had not prepared anything for this prayer time.

That's not like me at all. I'm a planner. So, of course, I started to panic. I frantically searched through my Bible to find something … anything … I could share that would inspire the group and start our day off right. But I came up with nothing.

I said, "Okay, God, you're going to have to show up *big time* today because I have no idea what I'm supposed to say!" Within seconds, in my spirit, I heard Jeremiah 32.

Now, let me back up a bit. My favorite verse, my life verse, is Jeremiah 29:11:

> "'For I know the plans I have for you,' declares the LORD, 'plans to prosper you and not to harm you, plans to give you hope and a future.'"

I've loved that verse for years. It's provided hope to me in some tough times. It's plastered all over my office, on coffee mugs (like the one I mentioned earlier), t-shirts, you name it. I *know* that verse!

I'm embarrassed to say it, but I don't think I had ever read anything else in Jeremiah *other* than my favorite verse. So, when I heard Jeremiah 32, I figured maybe I had heard wrong. But I figured I'd check it out anyway.

As I was flipping to find Jeremiah, I felt more confirmation that I wasn't supposed to read Jeremiah 32, but rather 30:2. So I did, and I couldn't believe my eyes!

To my amazement, Jeremiah 30:2 says,

> *"This is what the LORD, the God of Israel, says: Write in a book all the words I've spoken to you."*

Wow! Here we are at *Book Bound*, where soon-to-be authors gather to write their books. And this verse—the one I had *never* read before but felt God leading me to read the morning of this devotion—summed up *why* we should write ... and it's not about a book. It's about our story, and we're to use it to glorify God.

We need to record His faithfulness and all the things He's done for us. We need to share these stories to inspire, equip, and encourage the Body of Christ.

> ❝
> **We need to share these stories to inspire, equip and encourage the Body of Christ.**
> ❞

After the devotional, several attendees came to me and said that this one session meant more to them than the entire three days at the conference. The revelation from so many was that their stories were not about *them*. They were about *Him*, and we *must* share them in order to impact others. There was a collective realization amongst everyone: If we are the "light of the world," then we need to do what lights are created to do—*shine!* And when we shine, we're merely reflecting His light … the light of the SON.

MY "BOOK BOUND" STORY

One of those attendees was Tracy Frederick. Here's her story, in her own words:

> *A few years ago, I heard a voice that said, "I want you to write a book, and the name should be 'Meet My Friend Jesus.'" It was the familiar voice, but was it God? I wasn't sure. So, I thought, "Why not?" As I began writing, a few more details were revealed: it should be a small book, three chapters. And how about the color purple?*

> *I began writing the book, describing Jesus as my friend. After chapter three, I heard another voice that said, "Who are you to think that you could write a book? People are going to think you are a Jesus freak. What do you know about Jesus? Don't write this book."*

> *I knew this voice; it was mine! So of course, I listened to that voice too and filed the book somewhere deep in my computer.*

> *But I still had this burning desire to write a book, just not that book! I was introduced to Michelle Prince and her Book Bound Seminar. I went with a plan to write another book.*

> *After the first day, I had my book mapped out and shared it with the group. That night, when going over the day's events, I heard the familiar voice ask, "What about that other book?" I immediately replied, "I'm not here to write that book!"*

The next day, several times I heard the same phrase over and over. "What about that other book?" Through gritted teeth, I once again gave my statement that I was not here to write that book!

The final day of Book Bound was a Sunday morning. Over half of the attendees gathered in a circle for prayer led by Michelle. She then asked if anyone wanted to share their thoughts.

The man sitting directly across from me had my full attention as he talked about an article written by his friend. He proclaimed it to be a great read and told us the name was My Friend Jesus! *Chills ran down my spine; I slumped in my chair, and I silently said to myself, "You are talking to me, aren't you?"*

A woman stood up—her name is LeTesha Wheeler— and I will never forget the words that tumbled out of her mouth: "Sometimes God just wants us to be obedient. We don't have to know why. We don't have to have all the answers. We just need to obey."

My next thought was, "God, you are talking to me."

His reply was, "Yes, and if you write this book out of obedience to me, it will set the precedent for the rest of the books you **will** *write."*

I replied, "I'm in!"

I stood up and told Michelle and the group that I needed to change the book that I was going to write. Michelle's words to me were, "Tracy, I will help you write any book you want to write."

I had already signed up with Michelle the afternoon before to write my other book. What I didn't realize was that I had agreed to write a small book that she calls a business card book. You see, the plan had been laid out long before I heard the voice. My little book has a place in this world. It was no accident that I showed up at Book Bound. My experience there reminded me that what I have to say is important. I now encourage others to listen to the voice that speaks to them.

Tracy Frederick
Author, *Meet My Friend Jesus*

Tracy has graciously agreed to give everyone a free copy of her book, *Meet My Friend Jesus*. To get your copy, go to www.tracyrfrederick.com

> **As believers, we need to document all that we are learning and experiencing with God in our own lives.**

This story is just one of the many amazing stories that came out of that event. Others shared with me how they were led by God to attend this event despite major health, travel, and financial obstacles. Many impactful books came out of those three days. It was definitely a time of rebirth for many, and God showed up in a BIG way! Thank you, Jesus!

As believers, we need to document all that we are learning and experiencing with God in our own lives. When we write these reflections down, it allows us to go back over time and see all the wonderful blessings God has provided us.

My Conversations With God

You'd think this revelation at my conference in 2019 of *why* we're supposed to tell our stories would have sunk in sooner, but it took another year for me to really see how I could help people connect with God in a more personal way.

In the winter of 2020, I went through a ten-week small group program at my church called *Rooted*. It was a life-changing experience that further confirmed my beliefs and God's faithfulness in our lives. Each week, ten women gathered to review the weekly lesson and discuss what we learned. Then, each woman would share their personal faith story with the group.

The stories were powerful. I knew all the women in my group before joining *Rooted*, but after hearing their stories, the stories we don't always share, I felt even more connected to them.

When the time came to share my story, I was surprised at how nervous I felt. After all, I speak and write books for a living, and I tell my story all the time. But this was a different kind of story. It was the back story, most of which I'm sharing with you in this book. And it was the first time that I opened myself up and talked about my intimate walk with God.

The central theme of my story was God's faithfulness and how I connect with Him through writing and journaling. That didn't seem too out of the ordinary to me. After all, I'd been doing it my whole life. But a few of the women commented that they had never connected to God through journaling.

That surprised me. I assumed everyone did that. Then, a couple days later, I got the "download."

I call it a download because there are times I hear so clearly from God that I can't take any of the credit. It's all Him. It's as if He's downloading something important onto my "hard drive," and all I can do is grab a pen and jot down what I'm hearing.

Very clearly, I heard God tell me to create a prayer journal for these ladies. It would be simple, and it would follow a formula to help them connect with God through writing. It would include personalized scripture on every page of the journal to encourage them through God's Word.

I immediately got to work, and I was able to have it published in time to give it to them as a gift for our graduation. I guess that's one of the perks of owning my own publishing company. I called it *My Conversations With God Personalized P.R.A.Y.E.R. Journal.*

JOURNAL THROUGH P.R.A.Y.E.R.

You can connect with God through writing and journaling too. Start by recording His faithfulness and your brokenness in a daily journal. There is no right or wrong way to journal. The key is to open yourself up and write whatever is on your heart.

> **There is no right or wrong way to journal. The key is to open yourself up and write whatever is on your heart.**

Allow the Holy Spirit to speak to you. Record what you hear. It's amazing how God has used writing to speak to me all these years. I have a hunch He'll do the same for you.

I'd like to share with you the simple formula that I shared with my church group. It follows the acronym **P.R.A.Y.E.R.**

P - PRAISE
R - REPENT
A - ASK
Y - YIELD
E - ENTER
R - RESPOND

P – PRAISE

"I will give thanks to you, Lord, with all my heart; I will tell of all your wonderful deeds. I will be glad and rejoice in you; I will sing the praises of your name, O Most High."
(Psalm 9:1-2)

Thank God for all His wonderful deeds. Thank Him for His goodness, His power, His mercy, His wisdom, and love. Write out your praises to God and give glory to your Father Who is faithful to you.

> **There is so much to be grateful for if we take the time to notice all the beauty and blessings around us.**

There is so much to be grateful for if we take the time to notice all the beauty and blessings around us. The red cardinal caring for its babies in a nest outside your kitchen window. The warm glow of the sun rising on the horizon. The giggles and smiles from your kids. The random kindness from a stranger.

Praise God for your individual uniqueness, talents, skills, passions, and the ability to make your own decisions! It's easy to recognize all the wonderful things God is doing in our lives when we stop, take notice, and actively thank Him for His blessings.

R – REPENT

"If we claim to be without sin, we deceive ourselves and the truth is not in us. If we confess our sins, he is faithful and just and will forgive us our sins and purify us from all unrighteousness."
(1 John 1:8-9)

Recognize and repent for your sins. Let God know, through your journaling, about the areas of your life where you have fallen short and need forgiveness. God already knows your sins, but it's in the act of repentance that we come into agreement with God, thus honoring and creating a closer, more intimate relationship with Him.

I could write a million books listing my sins and shortcomings, and it still wouldn't cover them all. But thankfully, God is a good Father. He is willing to forgive and love us, even when we don't deserve it.

In my life, especially over the last couple of decades, I've often had to beg for forgiveness because I was "chasing" the wrong things. As I shared earlier, God clearly told me to "Stop! Stop chasing the wind. Stop chasing what is not My plan. Trust Me."

When I stopped *chasing the wind*, I became more aware of my calling and the plans He has for me. Plans to prosper me and not to harm me. Plans to give me a future and hope.

> When I stopped chasing the wind, I became more aware of my calling and the plans He has for me. Plans to prosper me and not to harm me. Plans to give me a future and hope.

Sometimes, it is not about what we do, but about what we *don't do* in life that matters most. Sometimes, we can get lost in our own comforts or the comforts of the world. Sometimes, we get tied up and misguided by the ways of the world, like chasing the dollar, fads, or fame. If this is you, don't worry. You can have instant relief when you redirect your focus on His purposes and REPENT!

We are being called for so much more than we can imagine—to be an example for others, to stand up and stand out!

A – ASK

"Ask and it will be given to you, seek and you will find; knock and the door will be opened for you. For everyone who asks receives; the one who seeks finds; and the one who knocks, the door will be opened."
(Matthew 7:7-8)

Ask God for the things you desire. God is a good and loving Father Who takes delight in His children. He wants to give us the desires of our heart, but first we must ask. Write out and ask God for what you want and need—but also know that God will only give you what He believes is best for you.

THE PRINCIPLE OF 2 CHAIRS

One of my favorite books in recent years is *2 Chairs: The Secret that Changes Everything* by author Bob Beaudine.

In it, Bob recognizes the harsh reality that in this life we will experience trouble and heartache. But to help believers overcome these challenges and difficult situations, Bob encourages readers with Jesus' words from John 16:33 NIV:

"In this world you will have trouble.
But take heart! I have overcome the world."

Even before His crucifixion, Jesus is declaring His victory! Because our identity is found in Him and His resurrection. And conquering death gets to be our prize as well!

2 Chairs teaches a reflection practice that can be summarized in three simple questions:

- *Does God know your situation?*
- *Is it too hard for Him to handle?*
- *Does He have a good plan for you?*

Obviously, God knows your situation. He knows *everything about you*. And if He can defeat the grave, you can trust that nothing is too hard for Him to handle. Finally, the answer to the third question, *"Does He have a good plan for you?"* is an unequivocal *yes*!

To know what that plan is, you first must ASK.

Y – YIELD

"Call to me and I will answer you and tell you great and unsearchable things you do not know."
(Jeremiah 33:3)

To yield means to listen. After you have given praise to God for His goodness, repented for your sins, and asked for His help, now is the time to be quiet and *listen*. God speaks to us, and when you regularly take time to listen, you will hear His voice and feel His grace.

I tend to hear God's voice the loudest when I am by the ocean. Something about the vast ocean waters makes me feel so alive. I feel overwhelmed by the sheer size of the ocean and become humbly aware of my insignificance.

I also tend to hear God's voice most when I am writing, as I've mentioned. That's why I pair my journaling time with my listening time. It's like the very act of typing words or writing my thoughts out makes me connect so much closer to the heart of God.

So, after you ask God to speak to you, prepare yourself in a way that will allow you to best listen to Him and His response to you. You may be thinking that you are so busy, and it is a challenge to make time to do ANYTHING for yourself, let alone have quiet time with God. My response to this is simple. You must *take* the time and *make* the time for Him. He is the answer. He has the answers for you!

E – ENTER

"This is what the Lord, the God of Israel, says: Write in
a book all the words I have spoken to you."
(Jeremiah 30:2)

Now that you've heard God speak to you, enter it in your journal. Write it down.

It's amazing the revelation that God will reveal to us when we take the time to listen. It's equally important that we don't just *hear* His voice, but that we *record* it, too. Keeping a record of what God has said to you is a great way to build your relationship with God. When you can go back and see how faithful God has been to you, you will be grateful and strengthened in your faith.

I love going back to re-read my journal entries, especially the times when I was going through something heavy, and I pleaded with God to help me. In the moment, and even in the days or months after, I couldn't see how God was moving in my life or that things were improving. But because I documented the journey, time and time again I could see how faithful God was to me, how much He loves me, and how consistently He answered my prayers and provided revelation at just the right time.

It's easy to forget all the wonderful things God does for us. Writing it down will help you to see how much He listens to you, loves you, and is working on your behalf.

R – RESPOND

"Anyone who loves me will obey my teaching. My Father will love
them, and we will come to them and make our home with them."
(John 14:23)

Whatever God is telling you to do, it's time to respond ... to obey. If you obey the Lord's commands, He will give you the courage, strength, and grace to complete any task. And in doing so, your obedience will be a sincere act of worship to Him.

Once you've received your marching orders from God, it's best to not delay in your obedience. Doing so can lead to sin and muffle the voice of God from giving you any more direction.

When we stop and listen to what God is telling us, and then write it down, He will make the path clear on *how* to respond ... how to obey.

While I was still searching and unsure of my next steps several years ago, I clearly heard God telling me to do three things. The first was to get baptized.

As I mentioned already, I was a strong believer most of my life. I was baptized in the Catholic church as a baby and felt very strongly that I didn't need to do it again. That is, until God showed me why I should get baptized ... again.

Jesus modeled baptism for His followers as an act of obedience. It is a symbol of faith and a public declaration. Much like a wedding ring signifies a sacred relationship between spouses, baptism symbolizes our relationship with God. Baptism is an outward profession of an inward decision. Realizing this, I not only wanted to honor and obey God's wishes, but I also wanted to re-establish and profess my commitment to Him. And so, at thirty-nine years old, that's exactly what I did.

The second thing He told me to do was to buy a certain family member a Bible. I found this strange, as this person already had *many* Bibles and clearly didn't need another one. But after many months of thinking I had heard incorrectly, I decided to buy this person a beautiful new Bible with their name engraved on the front. This gift had a profound impact on this person, and I saw first-hand how God moved in their life immediately following.

The last thing God told me to do was write a book. You already know that story, and let's just say I'm sure glad I did!

He's Calling You by Name

Are you answering His call for you and your life? If you long to be fully known and experience God more intimately, then I encourage you to journal as an expression of prayer. God is so faithful. His promises are true, and when you record your praise, prayers, and petitions to your Heavenly Father, there is transformation in the revelation of His great faithfulness.

My prayer for you is that you use writing to strengthen and deepen your relationship with God. By documenting your story, I pray that you see the wonder and awesome power of Almighty God at work in your life. He loves you. He's faithful to you, and He's calling you by name.

For more information or support on your journey, go to www.SHINEThroughYourStory.com, where you'll find helpful resources, like *My Conversations With God P.R.A.Y.E.R. Journals.*

Chapter Eight

S.H.I.N.E – Encourage and Equip Others

*"Therefore encourage one another and build each other up,
just as in fact you are doing."*
(1 Thessalonians 5:11)

N ow that you know how to *Sow Your Seeds of Greatness, Honor Your Story, Identify What's Holding You Back,* and you fully understand that *Now Is the Time to Write Your Story,* there is one last step to take for you to fully *SHINE Through Your Story.* You have to **Encourage and Equip Others** to do the same.

> If we truly want to help others, we must get comfortable sharing our story and using our God-given gifts so that we can illuminate our inner lights onto others.

It's easy to underestimate all of our gifts, talents, potential, and the enormous opportunity we have to make a difference in this world. But if we truly want to help others, we must get comfortable sharing our story and using our God-given gifts so that we can illuminate our inner lights onto others.

It is the differences in our stories that allow others to relate to us and give us an opportunity for building trust with people to share the story of Jesus. Yet, we are united in the overarching mission. We all have a part to play in the *big story*.

Our stories may not matter to *everyone*, but I can guarantee that your story matters to *someone*. And it matters a whole lot to God. He gives us our desires, dreams, and goals because He is a good and loving Father who wants to bless His children and see us succeed—however we define it.

YOUR STORY IS A GIFT – GIFTS ARE MEANT TO BE SHARED

When we share our story with others, they will benefit from it too. Our stories give hope to those who are struggling. They give encouragement to the downtrodden. They give insight and instruction to those looking for wisdom.

No one person is better than another, but some people are further along the path you may want to be on. They have much to teach you. Consider these people fellow travelers on this journey called life.

> **Our story is not about us. It's about how God is using us to do extraordinary things in the lives of others – great, glorious, wonderful things.**

They know the lay of the land, and they can show you the way. They have learned lessons that can be shared to help those who are still trying to make their own path. And you can be one of these people who shares their story with others.

Our story is not about us. It's about how God is *using* us to do extraordinary things in the lives of others—great, glorious, wonderful things.

For a long time, I felt like sharing my story made it all about *me*. In fact, in the first few versions of this manuscript I left out many personal (and vulnerable) stories. Why? Because I felt like those extra details made it seem like I was being self-seeking, and making it too much about me, and not God. But then a true friend gave me some straight talk and called me out on it.

Here I am telling you to share your story—even the not so good parts—but then I attempt to write this book while glossing over and avoiding going too deep with my own story, my real story: the backstory. Ouch! That's what my friend pointed out to me, and she was right. I was playing it safe. I was playing small and leaving no room for God to be glorified through my stories. Thankfully, my friend set me straight, and I added my stories back into the manuscript so you can see the real me.

> " Life is too short to just "get by" and be ordinary. We were created for more. We were made to be extraordinary because we are made in the image of God. We are meant to shine. "

See, even when we know what to do, it doesn't mean we always do it. But life is too short to just get by and be ordinary. We were created for more. We were made to be *extraordinary* because we are made in the image of God. We are meant to shine. Not just to shine *our* lights, but to shine *His light* through us.

SO, HOW DO WE ENCOURAGE AND EQUIP OTHERS?

Each believer has a unique role to play in the world. When God's Holy Spirit dwells in you, He equips you with special gifts that are meant to be your ministry to others.

That's why it's so important to first identify what gifts, talents, and *seeds of greatness* that are already within you. Then you will be ready to start giving them away.

Beyond just our natural abilities and strengths, all believers are also equipped with spiritual gifts. And in Romans, the Apostle Paul says we are to serve God by serving others with our spiritual gifts:

"For by the grace given me I say to every one of you: Do not think of yourself more highly than you ought, but rather think of yourself with sober judgment, in accordance with the faith God has distributed to each of you. For just as each of us has one body with many members, and these members do not all have the same function, so in Christ we, though many, form one body, and each member belongs to all the others. We have different gifts, according to the grace given to each of us. If your gift is prophesying, then prophesy in accordance with your faith; if it is serving, then serve; if it is teaching, then teach; if it is to encourage, then give encouragement; if it is giving, then give generously; if it is to lead, do it diligently; if it is to show mercy, do it cheerfully."
(Romans 12: 3-8)

Every child of God is filled with the power of the Holy Spirit, specifically gifted to play a unique and powerful role in the world. When you understand that you can serve others with your story *and* your spiritual gifts, you will become unstoppable!

DISCOVERING YOUR SPIRITUAL GIFTS

Spiritual gifts are not our own talents or skills. They are the grace of God within us, empowering us to match our deep passions with the world's needs. When we live our spiritual gifts at home, at work, and in the community, we extend the blessing and healing of the Body of Christ to the world.

Before we can use our gifts effectively, we need to understand what they are. It's important to open ourselves up to the power of the Holy Spirit to deepen our understanding of our gifts, strive to develop and strengthen them, and seek to employ them everywhere we go.

Earlier, I shared with you my story about working in Corporate America and having the desire to make a difference. There were three words that frequently came to mind as I thought about my future. The words were ***motivate, inspire, and encourage***. I didn't know *how* I could do this, but I desperately wanted to do something that would motivate, inspire, and encourage other people.

A couple of years ago, I took a spiritual gifts assessment. The results were eye-opening and further confirmed what I already believed God was calling me to do back when He first told me to "write" in 2008.

After taking the spiritual gifts assessment, the survey results said that my #1 gift was the gift of exhortation. I'm embarrassed to admit it, but I wasn't exactly sure what that word meant at the time. So, I looked it up online, and here's the first definition I found:

> **Exhortation** – the ability to counsel, **inspire, motivate, and encourage** and strengthen others in and through their efforts to live out God's will and calling as Christians in pain or pleasure, want or plenty.

Do you see it? When I read this description, those three words literally leapt off the page, and I began to cry … a happy cry.

My desire has always been to **motivate, inspire, and encourage** others, AND my gift—the gift that I did nothing to earn or create but was given to me by God—is to do exactly that.

He even used the exact same words to get this message through my thick skull. The order may have been different, but the point was clear. Amazing!

God is so good, and there are no coincidences. He lovingly gives us our desires, as well as our gifts, to bless us so that we can be a blessing to others.

> "
> He lovingly gives us our desires, as well as our gifts, to bless us so that we can be a blessing to others.
> "

You have gifts. You have a purpose, and we are all called to live our purpose and use our gifts so we can further the Kingdom of God. What do you think might be your spiritual gifts? Let the Holy Spirit lead you. Write whatever comes to mind.

My Spiritual Gifts Are …

....
....
....
....
....
....
....
....

If you're still not sure what your spiritual gifts might be, I encourage you to find an online assessment. I recently came across an assessment offered by the Denison Ministries, which you can find at www.WhatAreMySpiritualGifts.org. I suggest you try this one or find another. Either way, don't delay discovering, understanding, and applying your Spiritual Gifts.

The Power of Authority

In 2019, I released a book called, *The Power of Authority – How to Get the Revenue, Respect & Results You Deserve by Writing a Book*. In it, I share how business owners like doctors, lawyers, financial advisors, coaches, speakers, accountants, etc., can distinguish themselves in the marketplace by becoming authors. I share insights to my own book writing process, how to come up with a book topic, and options for publishing.

The title, *The Power of Authority*, is a play on words. You can't spell **authority without author**, so the book guides professionals through the process of sharing their stories in a book to build their professional authority.

But what if we have access to a different kind of authority? Maybe one we don't even know about or haven't fully discovered yet? Or worse, one we *do* know about but aren't yet using? As believers, we do have authority! And there is power in understanding and embracing this authority.

"I pray that the eyes of your heart may be enlightened in order that you may know the hope to which he has called you, the riches of his glorious inheritance in his holy people, and his incomparably great power for us who believe. That power is the same as the mighty strength he exerted when he raised Christ from the dead and seated him at his right hand in the heavenly realms, far above all rule and authority, power and dominion, and every name that is invoked, not only in the present age but also in the one to come. And God placed all things under his feet and appointed him to be head over everything for the church, which is his body, the fullness of him who fills everything in every way."
(Ephesians 1:18-23)

What is authority? Authority is delegated power. A policeman directing traffic is an authority to the cars he's directing because of the power given to him by a city. He doesn't have the physical authority to stop a car by his might, but his uniform and badge represent that we need to adhere to what he tells us to do for our own safety.

The same is true for believers. Remember in Chapter 6 when we talked about the Armor of God? We are given authority by God to fight the enemy not because we are stronger, smarter, or more spiritual, but because the authority given to Jesus was transferred to us the moment we first believed.

"I have given you authority to trample on snakes and scorpions and to overcome all the power of the enemy; nothing will harm you. However, do not rejoice that the spirits submit to you, but rejoice that your names are written in heaven."
(Luke 10:19-20)

We are the body of Christ, and we're His commissioned representatives here on earth, acting as His mouth, hands, and feet. Therefore, we must remain in Him to fully utilize the authority He's given us and carry out the tasks He's called us to do.

We shouldn't be amazed by this authority either, because Jesus said,

> *"Very truly I tell you, whoever believes in me will do the works I have been doing, and they will do even greater things than these, because I'm going to the Father."*
> (John 14:12)

As believers, we need to claim the authority we have in Christ. We are meant to share our stories and send forth disciples. And in doing so, we will shine our light.

A Text Message from God

Most of my adult life, I have taken scripture and added my name to it so that I could make it more personal for me. It started with Ephesians, then Psalms, and now I have hundreds of scriptures personalized just for me.

> *For I know the plans I have for you," declares the Lord, "plans to prosper you and not to harm you, plans to give you hope and a future.*
> (Jeremiah 29:11)

> *"Put on the full armor of God, Michelle, so that you can take your stand against the devil's schemes."*
> (Ephesians 6:11)

> *"For he will command his angels concerning you, Michelle, to guard you in all your ways."*
> (Psalm 91:11)

"Michelle, call on me in the day of trouble;
I will deliver you, and you will honor me."
(Psalm 50:15)

I love knowing that God is speaking directly to me through His Word, and I'm inspired and encouraged even more when I see my name inserted into the scripture.

Not long after I created the *My Conversations With God P.R.A.Y.E.R. Journal*, I was seeking an easier, more convenient way for my family and me to connect with God.

My family practically lives on their phones. So, it occurred to me that if I set up a daily text message with scripture, it would guarantee that my boys (and me) would be in God's Word every single day.

Since I love the personalized scripture so much, I decided to write out a couple hundred verses, personalized, but without changing the verse in any way.

I set these up in a text messaging service to automatically text each of us every morning. I even created a new contact in my phone with that text messaging number and assigned the contact as "God." So now, every morning I look at my phone and see that I have a text message from God. I can't tell you how much that brightens my day!

This started as something just for me and my family, but I'd love to invite you to join us in our daily inspiration as well. It may not be much, but I see this as one more way I can encourage and equip God's people to shine each and every day by starting in the Word.

> To experience personalized scripture, messaged to you
> every morning, **text CONNECT to 833-744-0510.**

You Are the Light of The World

When we listen, God will speak. When God speaks, He will inspire. What God inspires, He will bless. What God blesses, He'll equip you to do.

But always remember to Him be the glory and honor. Whatever God calls you to, it is meant for His purposes and for His glory—and not the glory of you or for the praises of other people.

Jesus speaks these words to His followers:

> *"You are the light of the world. A town built on a hill cannot be hidden. Neither do people light a lamp and put it under a bowl. Instead they put it on its stand, and it gives light to everyone in the house. In the same way, let your light **shine** before others, that they may see your good deeds and glorify your Father in heaven."*
> (Matthew 5:14-16)

But that's not always easy to do. I see this in countless people who want to shine, who want to serve God, but *something* inside of them continues to hold them back. We've covered it a bit already, but it's worth repeating because it's what holds people back the most. That *something* is fear.

> **When we release those fears and let our true light shine for all to see, that's when we inspire and motivate others to do the same.**

There is nothing so tragic as a person, full of light, holding back for fear of what other people may think. We think we're being humble, but really, we're hiding behind our own fears and insecurities. When we release those fears and let our true light shine for all to see, that's when we inspire and motivate others to do the same. It's not selfish to shine; it's merely living out our faith for others to see.

DO IT AFRAID

Sharing my story hasn't always been easy for me. Even now, it's not easy. As I shared in chapter 6, this book has been "in the works" for several years now. God told me to write it, gave me clarity as to what to say, and yet, I procrastinated and hesitated to bring it to life. Why? Fear!

The fear of sharing my personal journey with God, the intimate details of how He's worked through my life, and the lessons I learned along the way (many of which were hard). The fear of sharing my faith, my brokenness, and my insecurities. The fear of opening myself up to criticism and judgment. The fear of really being seen for who I am, not just who I want to be. All those fears and more kept me from moving forward with this manuscript. But, even with fear, I press forward—because I know how important it is for me to share my story. Maybe it's for you. Maybe my story will inspire you to tell your story, too. More importantly, I look forward to what new aspects telling my story will unlock in my own life.

So, I get it! I know how hard it is to open yourself up and let people into the story of your life. But I also know how essential it is because, ultimately, it serves a bigger purpose. It serves His purpose. It's like the title of a book I once read: As author Susan Jeffers writes, we need to *Feel the Fear and Do It Anyway.* Let fear fuel you to press on and not hold you back. Use it to motivate you beyond your imagination.

> **Let fear fuel you to press on and not hold you back. Use it to motivate you beyond your imagination.**

Another thing I learned about fear is that it's a lie fed to us by a liar. This liar only wants to steal, kill, and destroy us (John 10:10). He's roaming around like a lion, waiting to devour us and stop us from shining our lights. But we don't have to let him. If you also struggle with fear and anxiety, then ask God to fill you with faith and cast out the fear that was deposited by the enemy. This enemy has no authority over you. After all, you are a chosen child of God.

> *"But the Lord Is faithful, and he will strengthen*
> *you and protect you from the evil one."*
> (2 Thessalonians 3:3)

Fear is the opposite of faith, and you can't have both at the same time. It's one or the other, so you have to choose. Will you choose fear or faith? Light or darkness? Life or death? I have no doubt you'll make the right choice.

Fear Not

The Bible tells us many times over that God is always with us. Here are a few Bible verses to remind us of this truth and to be fearless:

> *"Have I not commanded you? Be strong and courageous. Do not be frightened,*
> *and do not be dismayed, for the Lord your God is with you wherever you go."*
> (Joshua 1:9)

> *"Fear not, for I am with you; be not dismayed, for I am your God; I will*
> *strengthen you, I will help you, I will uphold you with my righteous right hand."*
> (Isaiah 41:10 NKJV)

> *"Be strong and courageous. Do not fear or be in dread of them, for it is the*
> *Lord your God who goes with you. He will not leave you or forsake you."*
> (Deuteronomy 31:6 ESV)

> *"Teaching them to observe all that I have commanded you. And*
> *behold, I am with you always, to the end of the age."*
> (Matthew 28:20 ESV)

*"For I am sure that neither death nor life, nor angels nor rulers,
not things present nor things to come, nor powers, nor height nor
depth, nor anything else in all creation, will be able to separate
us from the love of God in Christ Jesus our Lord."*
(Romans 8:38-39 ESV)

*"Even though I walk through the valley of the shadow of death, I will not
fear, for you are with me; your rod and your staff, they comfort me."*
(Psalm 23:4 ESV)

YOU ARE NOT ALONE

To Encourage & Equip others, we must remember that we can't do it alone. And, as these scriptures remind us, we are never really alone because God is always with us. On our own, we can't do much, but with God we can do all things through Him who gives us strength (Philippians 4:13).

When we focus on shining our light in order to help others, God will be gloried in the process. Because of this, He will equip you to shine for His purposes. I believe we are made in the image of God so that we can shine as brightly as possible to reflect His love and faithfulness onto others. Because of His goodness, we are now equipped to go out to encourage and equip other believers to do the same. Together, we can bring light into this world of darkness. Shine on!

Chapter Nine

Step Into Your Greatness Now

"Each of you should use whatever gift you have received to serve others,
as faithful stewards of God's grace in its various forms."
(1 Peter 4:10)

Your time to shine is now! Everything you need to shine, and shine BIG, is already within you. You were created with gifts, talents, and unique abilities that no one else has. You have a purpose, and God is counting on you to discover, cultivate, and live out your purpose so that you can partner with Him and bring light to the world.

> God is counting on you to discover, cultivate, and live out your purpose so that you can partner with Him and bring light to the world.

If you gave a gift to your child, spouse, or friend, a gift that you knew would make their life better—give them more joy, fulfillment, happiness, and peace—but they refused to use it, would you be frustrated? I know I would be.

Yet, many of us refuse to acknowledge or accept the gifts that God has freely given to us. These gifts are a part of our purpose and the reason we are here on this earth. We didn't deserve them, or work for them.

They were given to us by a generous Father. If God gave you gifts, it's time to start using them.

A couple of years ago, before I started writing this book, I was thinking about what my next book should be about. I kept coming back to the phrase "Step Into Your Greatness Now." It was like that song that you cannot get out of your head and keep humming all throughout your day.

I already mentioned that one of my favorite quotes from Zig Ziglar is, *"Man was designed for accomplishment, engineered for success, and endowed with the seeds of greatness."* So, since I talked about *seeds of greatness* so much and loved the metaphor of planting, I bought the URL and was pretty certain that *Step Into Your Greatness Now* would be the title of my next book. Well, you already know it didn't make the final cut for the title of *this* book, but I still love that phrase. Who knows, maybe there is still a book with that title in my future!

As I was brainstorming ideas for a possible book, I started to research the word "greatness." Most of us have our own definitions or are familiar with how many people in the world define greatness. Usually, greatness is associated with a person's talents, abilities, strengths, or accomplishments. Others might say it's about power or climbing the ladder of success. If those definitions are accurate, then is striving for success and greatness too boastful or self-seeking?

I wanted to know how God defined "greatness." So, I grabbed my Bible, flipped to the back index to see if I could find any Bible verses that referenced the concept of greatness, and I found two that hit home for me:

"Jesus called them together and said, 'You know that those who are regarded as rulers of the Gentiles lord it over them, and their high officials exercise authority over them. Not so with you. Instead, whoever wants to become great among you must be your servant, and whoever wants to be first must be slave of all. For even the Son of Man did not come to be served but to serve, and to give his life as a ransom for many.'"
(Mark 10:42-45)

"The greatest among you will be your servant. For those who exalt themselves will be humbled, and those who humble themselves will be exalted."
(Matthew 23:11-12)

If the Bible tells us that true greatness can be defined as serving, and Jesus is the greatest servant of all, then we are to exemplify Jesus in our daily actions by serving others. But how? We serve others by sharing more of ourselves. We serve others by sharing our stories.

Inside of you, God has planted *seeds of greatness* with the intention for them to germinate, blossom, grow, and take root to produce fruit that will be a blessing to others. Your story, your fruit, will benefit those who need encouragement, hope, and love. God gifted you with your story to serve Him and His children.

> **Inside of you, God has planted seeds of greatness with the intention for them to germinate, blossom, grow, and take root to produce fruit that will be a blessing to others.**

WOMEN OF LEGACY

Recently I attended the Women of Legacy Summit & Reunion in Washington D.C.. *Women of Legacy* is founded by Jackie Green, co-founder of Museum of the Bible. Its purpose is to help women discover and leave a legacy of faith. I'm honored to be included with such an amazing, spirit-led group of women committed to leaving a legacy that glorifies God and ripples through eternity.

I was initially invited to become a *Women of Legacy* member in 2018, so this most recent event was our reunion to reconnect and interact with fellow *Women of Legacy* and leaders from around the country. It was so inspiring, and I'm more passionate now than ever to continue to help believers share their stories of God's love and faithfulness in their lives.

One of the speakers at the Reunion was Virginia Prodan, author of *Saving My Assassin*. Virginia was born and raised in Romania and was an attorney under a communist regime. She spent most of her life searching for the truth. When she finally found it in the pages of the most forbidden book in all of Romania, Virginia accepted the divine call to defend Christians against unjust persecution in an otherwise ungodly land. For this act of treason, she was kidnapped, beaten, tortured, placed under house arrest, and came within seconds of being executed by an assassin. But thankfully, she lived to tell her story.

I was inspired by Virginia's courage and confidence to stand on God's promises, even in the face of an assassin. It encouraged me to also choose faith over fear and stand firm in the promises found in Psalm 91:4

> *"He will cover you with his feathers, and under his wings you will find refuge; his faithfulness will be your shield and rampart."*

Because Virginia shared her story at this event, I was reminded that God is our protector and our provider. He will direct our steps and show us the way if we will listen. We simply need to have faith, resist fear, ask for guidance, and take the first step. I needed that reminder. Maybe you do too. If God is calling you to share your story, then He'll help you to tell it—but you need to do your part and take action to share it now.

ARISE, SHINE

I love to watch the sun rise. There is something magical about seeing the sun burst through the horizon and turn the complete darkness of night into the bright light of day. No matter how many times I've seen it emerge, it still takes my breath away.

Just the other day, I was driving to an early meeting, and out of the darkness I could see the sun on the horizon about to break through. I pulled my car over to the side of the road so I wouldn't miss it. I watched the beauty of the light shine out from the darkness and into a new day. A minute or two before, it was pitch black. I could only see the road in front of me because of my car headlights, but now everything was illuminated, and I no longer needed them to see.

I believe God is calling us to do the same. God wants us to arise and emerge from our own darkness of insecurity, fear, lack, and doubt. He wants us to shine our light, which is the light of Christ rising upon us, and illuminate the world.

> **God wants us to arise and emerge from our own darkness of insecurity, fear, lack and doubt.**

"*Arise, shine, for your light has come, and the glory of the LORD rises upon you. See, darkness covers the earth and thick darkness is over the peoples, but the LORD rises upon you and his glory appears over you.*" (Isaiah 60:1-2)

This verse is such an encouragement to me, and I hope it is for you too. No matter how many difficult seasons you've been through, no matter how many times you've fallen down or experienced disappointments, God is telling you that your light has come! His glory covers you and enables you to shine His light for all the world to see.

Don't Wait

I want to tell you about my friend "Tom." Tom was in his mid-forties and appeared to be leading a happy, successful life. He spent a lot of time taking care of himself by eating right, exercising, and spending time with his family. He also carved out personal time to relax. He worked hard to balance his life between career and family, and his kids seemed to be very happy and well-adjusted.

But at Tom's annual physical, which he had skipped for the past four years, his doctor found a something unusual but assured Tom that it was probably nothing to worry about, but just to be sure, he sent a sample to the lab for further analysis.

Tom and his wife spent three anxious days waiting for the results. When the doctor finally called, he requested that Tom schedule another appointment to see him.

Because his doctor had asked him to come in for another visit, Tom perceived it to be serious. He and his wife prepared for the worst, but nothing could have prepared them for the news they heard that day.

Tom had cancer, and it was already in its advanced stages. The doctor told Tom he had approximately six months to live.

Tom spent several days going through the natural grieving process. First, he was in disbelief, and then he was overcome by unbearable sadness about leaving his family. This was followed by anger that such a tragic thing could be happening to him.

Finally, he understood that this was something he couldn't stop by complaining about it. So, he decided to take action.

Tom spent the next six months loving his wife and kids more than he had during their entire time together. He showered them with attention and let them know how much they meant to him. He prayed more than he ever had before, asking God to take care of his family when it was time for him to go.

Tom also spent time doing the things he loved. One of those activities was writing. After the kids were asleep, Tom wrote down all the things he wanted to say to them as their dad. He told stories about when they were babies, and he wrote about the fun trips and vacations they'd had through the years.

He wrote about the future as well, and he gave them advice and wisdom that he'd hoped to pass down as they grew. Since there was a chance he wouldn't be with them during those times, he put it in writing for them to read when they were ready.

Tom died six-and-a-half months after the doctor told him the terrible news. The family was obviously devastated, but there was also a sense of peace and gratitude for the quality time they'd been able to spend with their dad and husband during those final months.

Close to the end of Tom's life, he told his wife that he was actually grateful for this prognosis of only having six months to live. He said that without it, he would have never experienced the joy of *really living*.

Tom truly led by example in his last days. He was a light to others when he could have been angry, reclusive, needy, depressed, defeating, and self-absorbed. He could have given up on life, but he chose to live to the fullest until his last breath. It is how he lived and how he responded to adversity that created more shine in my life and inspired me to shine a spotlight on him in this book.

WHAT ARE YOU WAITING FOR?

What if the doctor told you that you had only six months to live? What would you do? How would you act? What would be the most important things you would want to accomplish?

No one wants to think their time is up tomorrow, or the day after. But the truth is, we all have a prognosis of death. We are all going to die one day and leave our loved ones behind.

Given the same circumstances as Tom, undoubtedly, we would also make the best use of our time. *But what about now?* Why not start living that way now?

Life can be so busy. Even if we have some down time, we can easily fill it up with "stuff." But let's face it: life will *always* be busy. Before I got married and had kids, I thought I was too busy to take on anything else. Life was full. Yet, I was able to partner with my husband and bring two perfect children into the world. I handled all the responsibilities of being a mother and wife, all while continuing to build an ever-growing career. We can and always will make room for our priorities if we choose to do so. What are you prioritizing today?

There will always be an errand to run or an obligation to fulfill. So, if you're going to be busy anyway, then make the decision to shine through your story *while* you're busy.

LEAVE A LEGACY WITH YOUR STORY

> **We can and always will make room for our priorities if we choose to do so. What are you prioritizing today?**

We may never really know how much our story will impact another person's life until we're gone. It's easy to take our story, our life, for granted and think that it doesn't matter *that* much. It does.

I've been to many funerals—and I'm sure you have too—packed to the brim with people telling stories of what a difference that person made in their lives. Story after story of how they were inspired, encouraged, or moved by their life.

What's tragic is that many people go to their grave without really knowing that their lives mattered. If only they knew how their life story would leave such a beautiful legacy.

Here's what I know ... and its good news. You have the ability to change people's lives with your story. You can use the gifts, talents, passions, and experiences that God has given you to make a difference for others.

You've been given everything you need to encourage and equip others with the story of your life. Now is the time to take hold of the opportunity in front of you. To boldly step out of your comfort zone, break through whatever limiting beliefs are holding you back, and claim all the blessings and promises that God has in store for you.

God gave you the story of your life for a reason—for a purpose—and that purpose is to serve *His* greater purpose *through* you and to fight the big fight against the enemy's strongholds. What an awesome opportunity—but it's also a great responsibility that we need to take seriously, so I encourage you to start now.

You were created to make a difference, to shine your light, and to share your story. Your story is a gift, given to you by God and intended for a purpose. When you shine, He shines.

> **You were created to make a difference, to shine your light, and to share your story. When you shine, He shines.**

Friend, there's no time to waste. You've been called upon. It's time for you to *SHINE Through Your Story*! Don't overthink it or second guess yourself. I believe in you, and I know you can do this. It's your time to SHINE!

"Let it shine, let it shine, let it shine!"

For more resources on how you can SHINE, go to
www.SHINEThroughYourStory.com

or email us at
Support@SHINEThroughYourStory.com

ABOUT THE AUTHOR

Michelle Prince is a best-selling author, sought-after motivational speaker, and the CEO/Founder of Performance Publishing Group, a partner publishing company dedicated to making a difference ... one story at a time. Michelle knows that everyone has a story to tell, and she is passionate about helping them tell it for God's glory.

Michelle assists companies and individuals through her training and people-building solutions. She helps them ignite their passions, identify their talents, achieve balance, unlock potential, and be more productive, all so they can achieve abundant success in their personal and professional lives.

For information on Michelle's speaking,
corporate training, and people-building solutions, go to
www.MichellePrince.com
or
www.PrincePerformance.com

Or you can email us at
Support@MichellePrince.com

For information on how to publish your story, go to
www.PerformancePublishingGroup.com
or email
Support@PerformancePublishingGroup.com

Additional Books & Resources
from Michelle Prince

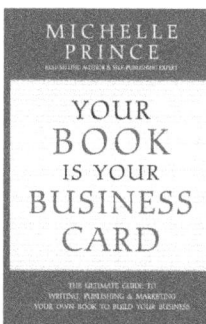

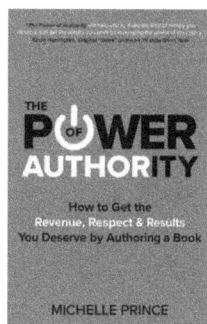

You can find these books and more at Amazon.com

www.ingramcontent.com/pod-product-compliance
Lightning Source LLC
Chambersburg PA
CBHW032054090426
42744CB00005B/219